THE ASIAN LINEUP

ICHIRO SUZUKI . . . Right fielder, Seattle Mariners, a budding superstar driven by his dream of playing in Yankee Stadium.

KAZUHIRO SASAKI . . . Rookie of the Year in 2000, also a Mariner, he led the American League in saves.

HIDEO NOMO . . . He threw a spring 2001 no-hitter for the Boston Red Sox, after pitching one earlier for the Los Angeles Dodgers.

HIDEKI IRABU . . . Former Yankee, now playing for Montreal.

TSUYOSHI SHINJO . . . Second Japanese nonpitcher signed to the majors, now playing in the Mets outfield.

WILL THEIR NAMES SOON BECOME AS FAMILIAR AS RIPKEN, GWYNN, PIAZZA, RANDY JOHNSON, RIVERA, AND PEDRO? FIND OUT IN . . .

BASEBALL SAMURAIS:
ICHIRO SUZUKI AND THE ASIAN INVASION

ALSO BY ROB RAINS

Mark McGwire: Home Run Hero

BASEBALL SAMURAIS

ICHIRO SUZUKI AND THE ASIAN INVASION

ROB RAINS

St. Martin's Paperbacks

BASEBALL SAMURAIS: ICHIRO SUZUKI AND THE ASIAN INVASION

Copyright © 2001 by Rob Rains.
Foreword copyright © 2001 by Rex Hudler.

Cover photo of Ichiro Suzuki copyright © Associated Press
Back cover photos of Hideo Nomo, Tsuyoshi Shinjo, and Kazuhiro Sasaki © Allsport

ISBN: 0-312-98257-7

Printed in the United States of America

St. Martin's Paperbacks edition / October 2001

St. Martin's Paperbacks are published by St. Martin's Press, 175 Fifth Avenue, New York, N.Y. 10010.

10 9 8 7 6 5 4 3 2 1

ACKNOWLEDGMENTS

The author would like to thank the many people who contributed to this project, including Brad Lefton, an expert on Japanese baseball; Mark Langill of the Los Angeles Dodgers; Chris Stathos of the Kansas City Royals; Steve Gietschier and Jim Meier at *The Sporting News*, all of the newspaper reporters who cover any Japanese player on a regular basis; Marc Resnick and George Witte of St. Martin's Press; and my family, Sally, B.J., and Mike, for their love and support.

ROB RAINS
JULY 2001

CONTENTS

FOREWORD

by Rex Hudler

One of the many get-well cards and letters I received when I was ill in April 2001 came from Ichiro Suzuki. It lifted my spirits and really pumped me up, as did hearing from all of my friends. The only difference about this letter was I had never met Ichiro.

When I played with the Yakult Swallows in Japan in 1993, Ichiro was playing with Orix. We never played against each other, but he told me in his letter how much he admired me for going to Japan and that I was one of the guys he looked up to because I came to Japan from the U.S. to play, accepting the challenge of learning their culture and adapting to their game.

Now, Ichiro and others are doing the same thing in our country, coming from Japan to play our game and learn our culture. It's brought a breath of fresh air to our game. It's great for our game and it's great that he has been so successful so quickly.

When you go to another country for nine months you are definitely challenged. Speaking from my personal experience, Ichiro will learn more about himself this year than he ever knew in Japan. He will absorb and learn. He is open-minded, and even though he was treated like a rock star in Japan, he has no ego. He is always thinking about his team, the Seattle Mariners, first, and that's one of the reasons he is fitting in so well in our game.

I learned during my year in Japan, as Ichiro and the other Japanese players are learning here, that baseball is a universal game. It has a language all its own. They play it with a different spice in Japan, and it is good for us to see that. It's not just America's game anymore. In Japan players are taught at an early age to control their emotions, but now these guys are letting those emotions show, and I think it's great.

I like the fact that Ichiro has so much confidence in his ability, as well he should. He has led every professional league where he has ever played in batting average, and it won't surprise me if he does it again this year.

He is a special player, and for Japan to let him come here and play takes a lot of pride. He knew what he was doing. It's been great for the Japanese people, for the Japanese game and the American game. There will be more coming.

The fact that Kazuhiro Sasaki and Tsuyoshi Shinjo also are doing so well for the Mariners and Mets respectively, and that Hideo Nomo has bounced back this year with Boston, just shows the depth of the talent that is playing in Japan. They don't have the pool of players to draw from that we have in this country, but it's a very good, high level of baseball and they are getting better all the time.

I learned how serious the Japanese are about baseball during my year with Yakult. Batting second in spring training, I missed one sign. I hit eighth the rest of the season, even though I hit .300, finished sixth in the league in batting, the only American in the top 10, and we won the championship.

I had come from the baseball promised land, in St. Louis, but that year in Japan opened up my whole person as a human being. I was living in a different culture, and even though I had been playing professional baseball for 17 years, it really pumped me up. It was a very valuable season for me, and I learned so much there, and my wife Jennifer and I will always cherish those memories.

I hope Ichiro, Kazuhiro, Tsuyoshi and the rest of the Japanese players have the same fond memories of the U.S. as I have of Japan.

After I returned to work as a broadcaster for the Angels following my illness, I was standing on the field in Seattle when Ichiro walked by me. I called out to him, and he kind of did a double take, then came right over. We hugged, and through his interpreter, I thanked him for his letter and his get-well wishes and told him how much it had meant to me. It showed me what a big heart he has.

Ichiro said he wanted to come to America and be successful in our game, and I think he's done that. I'm glad I had the chance to meet him, and I'm glad all Americans are getting a chance to watch him play this great game. He is a special player and a special person.

REX HUDLER

CHAPTER 1

A New Era

As Ichiro Suzuki walked to the plate in the seventh inning of the Seattle Mariners' opening day game against Oakland on April 2, it would have been natural for him to be a little nervous. Although he had won seven consecutive batting titles in Japan, his major league career was only six innings old. He had been to bat three times and still had not gotten the ball out of the infield.

The first position player from Japan ever to play in a major league game, Ichiro—already known in the United States only by his first name, the one on top of the number 51 on the back of his jersey—had prepared himself for the pressure and scrutiny he would be under. This game was being televised live back to Japan on two networks. Millions of people were watching. It was on the radio. Those who couldn't watch were listening. A record crowd had filled Safeco Field, many of the fans wearing Ichiro replica jerseys as they left their homes in the Seattle area's large Japanese community.

Despite his success in Japan, Ichiro knew there were people in both the United States and his homeland who doubted whether he could be a successful player in the major leagues. Others wondered too but were cheering and hoping that he would make it. He knew that for whatever reason, there probably were people rooting against him, hoping he would fail. He knew his career, or even his season, certainly would not be defined by what he did in his first game.

Inside, however, he hoped that this would be the at-bat when he would deliver his first major league hit. After all, the Mariners needed to rally. They trailed 4 to 2. Reliever T. J. Mathews was on the mound for the A's.

As television cameras rolled and thousands in the stands tried to snap a picture, Ichiro calmly bounced a single into center field for his first major league hit. The ball was taken out of play.

Ichiro could not help but hear the cheers as he stood on first base, but he forced his mind to concentrate on the task at hand—trying to win the game. He later scored on a hit by Edgar Martinez as the Mariners tied the game, then won it in the eighth. In that inning Ichiro contributed a key bunt single.

One of the players watching and cheering from the Seattle bullpen was relief pitcher Kazuhiro Sasaki, who only a year earlier had made his major league debut after a long career in Japan. With the Mariners ahead, he came out of the bullpen and retired the A's in the ninth to preserve the victory.

"I'm sure there will be some celebrations going

on," Ichiro said about the reaction to the win in Japan. "I was very glad I could contribute. I want to be here for a long time. What I felt tonight I will never forget."

Baseball has been played in Japan for almost as many years as it has been played in the United States. Nevertheless, it took more than a hundred years before Ichiro became the first Japanese non-pitcher to play in a major league game. The next day outfielder Tsuyoshi Shinjo made his debut with the New York Mets.

Both men faced not only the personal challenge of trying to succeed against the best players in the world but the added pressure of knowing an entire country was watching them.

"Imagine Mark McGwire going to Japan," said one Japanese television coordinator. "That's how big Ichiro is. It's big."

When Masanori Murakami became the first Japanese player in American baseball as a pitcher for the San Francisco Giants in 1964 and 1965, it was viewed as an anomaly. It was thirty years before another Japanese player tried to make the jump to the major leagues; Hideo Nomo joined the Los Angeles Dodgers in 1995.

Other pitchers have come since, with varying degrees of success. It takes more than just raw ability to make the cultural adjustment to living and working in another country.

Jim Colborn, now the pitching coach for the Dodgers and a former scout for the Mariners who was instrumental in persuading Sasaki and others to come to the major leagues, believes Nomo's success had a lot to do with changing the opinions of many Japanese players that they could he successful in the majors.

"I think the talent was always there," Colborn told the *Los Angeles Times*. "But you would ask a Japanese player in the 1990s if he was interested in playing in the majors and he would so 'no they are too big, too powerful.' They tended to be intimidated. Once they could make the comparison based on the performance of one of their own, many started to envision coming, and I think many more will make the jump. They are in the top one percent for dedication, determination and perseverance. Those are characteristics you can count on."

When the current generation of baseball stars was growing up, nobody talked about coming to the major leagues. Even in Japan, the U.S. professionals were called "major leaguers." Youngsters like Ichiro dreamed of one day growing up and playing in the Japanese league.

These youngsters, however, were just as dedicated—if not more so—than young boys growing up in California, Florida, or any other U.S. state who had a poster of their favorite player on their bedroom wall and went to bed dreaming of the day they would be starring for their favorite team.

The boys in Japan went to bed dreaming of playing for the Yomuri Giants or another Japanese team. Players for those teams were their heroes; those were the players the boys looked up to and aspired to be like, not Michael Jordan.

There is a story that apparently is true about Ichiro when he was a young boy. He would play catch and work out with his father on a daily basis. After he had returned home from school and completed his homework, his father would take him to the local batting cage. When Ichiro was able to master the fastest speed, his father asked the owner to turn the machine even faster. The owner said it would not go any faster, so Ichiro's father had his son move up to bat from a shorter distance, giving him less time to react to the pitch and making it seem as if it were coming faster.

There probably are similar stories about other Japanese youngsters, both those who decided to come to the United States to play in the major leagues and those who decided to remain in Japan.

What Ichiro accomplished in his first few months in the majors, however, can hardly be equaled by anyone.

He helped the Mariners to their best start in franchise history and to a double-digit lead in the AL West before the end of May. He was on pace to break the all-time record for most hits in a season, a record that had stood for eighty-one years. He was contending for the batting title. He was headed for the Rookie of the Year award and perhaps the Most Valuable Player trophy. And he became the first rookie since catcher Sandy Alomar Jr. in 1990 to be voted into the starting lineup for the All-Star game.

"He's caught the fancy of the public," said Seattle manager Lou Piniella. "He's their favorite and rightfully so. He's a dynamic kid. He's a professional in every sense of the word."

Seattle has had its share of stars in recent years. Randy Johnson pitched there. Ken Griffey Jr. patrolled the outfield and hit home runs. Most experts considered shortstop Alex Rodriguez the best player in the game.

None, however, was able to match Ichiro's sudden popularity. Only the most dedicated fans knew how good a player he had been in Japan, and even they didn't believe he would be able to be so good so quickly in the United States.

Opponents quickly found out that Ichiro could beat them with his bat, with either a single or a home run. He could beat them with speed, forcing infielders to adjust where they were playing so he would not be able to beat out a routine ground ball. He could beat them with his rocket arm, throwing strikes from deep in the outfield to cut down opposing runners. He could beat them with his glove, leaping over the wall to take away a would-be home run.

And perhaps most impressive, they learned he

could beat them with his head. Facing pitchers he had never seen before, except on videotape, he would make adjustments from at-bat to at-bat or even from pitch to pitch, forcing pitchers constantly to change how they tried to get him out.

That earned him the respect not only of his teammates but of his opponents and baseball fans in two countries.

"Ichiro could have come here with a big head, because he's like the Michael Jordan of Japan, but he's tried very hard to fit in," said relief pitcher Jeff Nelson of the Mariners.

Within the first week of the season, almost all of the nine Japanese players in the major leagues were fitting in just fine.

In New York, Shinjo starred in the Mets opener with an outstanding catch, scored two runs, and showed off his blazing speed. In Baltimore a couple of days later, Nomo pitched the second no-hitter of his career, for the Red Sox. Back in Seattle, in addition to Ichiro's heroics, Sasaki kept coming out of the bullpen to save games for the Mariners.

One of the most interested observers, not only that week but all season, has been Masanori Murakami, who frequently works the games of the current Japanese players for national radio and television broadcasts back to Japan.

As he thinks back to his games for the Giants more than thirty-five years ago, Murakami realizes how much closer the countries of Japan and the United States have come—because of baseball.

When the Red Sox came to Seattle in early May to face the Mariners, their pitching rotation just happened to fall so that Nomo was scheduled to start. When he faced off against Ichiro, fans in two countries—but particularly in Japan—sat riveted to their television screens.

When Nomo left Japan in 1995, he said he was looking for a new challenge. He found it in Los Angeles and the major leagues.

Ichiro said much the same thing when he left Japan after the 2000 season. He wasn't worried about relations between the two countries. He wasn't trying to be a pioneer. He didn't really see that he was going to be doing anything dramatically different from what he had been doing all his life and as a professional for nine years.

"I just want to play baseball," he said.

When he sits alone in his inner space in front of his locker in the Mariners' clubhouse before a game, away from the media distractions, he is thinking about only one thing: what he will do in that day's game that will help his team win.

That internal pressure to succeed might be as great as all of the external battles he faces on a daily basis.

Methodically rubbing a six-inch wooden stick up and down the sides and bottoms of his feet, Ichiro is relaxing. "It's for pressure points," he told *Sports Illustrated*.

When Ichiro says the only thing he misses about Japanese baseball is his dog, you believe him. You also know he means no disrespect to that country's game when he says it.

Japanese players, just like American professionals, need to have an appreciation of history and knowledge of the players who came before them if they are going to give the game its proper respect. Ichiro does that too.

He knows that he is in Seattle, playing in the major leagues, only because of the efforts of others. He won't forget.

CHAPTER 2

History of Japanese Baseball

As is the case with baseball history in the United States, there are several theories about who first brought the game from America to Japan. Most historical accounts give the credit to Horace Wilson, an American-born English and history teacher at Kaisei Gakko in Tokyo. He is said to have handed a bat and ball to his students in the 1870s. The Japanese quickly named the game *yakyu*, which, translated, means "field ball."

It was another American-born professor, Albert Bates, who is said to have organized the first formal game in 1873. Hiroshi Hiraoka, a railroad engineer who had studied in Boston, is credited with establishing the first team in Japan, the Shimbashi Athletic Club Athletics, in 1883.

The Japanese quickly began to pick up the finer points of baseball, at the same time American players were learning and developing skills half the world away. Culturally, the Japanese were developing more of an appreciation for the mental challenges baseball presented than the physical skills necessary to play the game successfully. Historian Robert Whiting, one of the experts on the history

of baseball in Japan, has said that the Japanese
found the one-on-one battle between pitcher and
batter similar in psychology to their native sumo
and martial arts. The game involved split-second
timing and a special harmony of mental and physical skills. That was one of the reasons the Japanese
Ministry of Education believed it was good for the
national character of its people and encouraged and
promoted the game's growth.

The game became especially popular among
younger players, and competitive games were
played at the high school and collegiate levels. The
annual national high school baseball tournament
was established in 1915; to this day it remains the
most popular sporting event each year in Japan.
Because of their background in the martial arts,
managers taught their players to play the game very
rigidly and seriously. It was said that managers often believed that if their players were not bleeding,
then they were not practicing hard enough.

The game was not universally popular, however.
Asahi Shunbun, an influential conservative newspaper, ran an editorial series titled "The Evil of
Baseball" in the early 1900s. The newspaper
quoted several leading Japanese educators who opposed the game. One physician was quoted as saying the "mental pressure" of playing baseball was
bad for personality development and also that
throwing a baseball could cause lopsided body development.

That theory was not picked up by others, however. One of the sport's leading proponents was Matsutara Shoriki, owner of another influential newspaper. He became known as "the great genius–father figure" of Japanese baseball. It was his idea to bring American stars to Japan on an all-star tour to play against local Japanese players. The first tour by a U.S. team was in 1908, when a group of reserves from the major leagues and Pacific Coast League players formed the traveling team. The U.S. squad won all seventeen games it played against a team of Japanese collegiate stars.

In 1913 the Chicago White Sox played four games in Japan as part of a world tour. Another group of backup players from the majors went to Japan in 1920, and in 1922 the Japanese team defeated the Americans for the first time.

The first tour featuring stars from the major leagues was in 1931, but Babe Ruth did not travel to Japan. The U.S. team went 17 to 0 on the trip.

Three years later Ruth did go to Japan as the U.S. major leaguers returned for an exhibition series. The U.S. team again won all eighteen games, and Ruth was the major star, hitting fourteen home runs in those eighteen games. That tour was so successful that it led to Shoriki founding Japan's first professional team later that year, the Great Japan Tokyo Baseball Club.

The locals had a chance to cheer when seventeen-year-old right-handed pitcher Eiji Sa-

wamura nearly won a game. He had a no-hitter
until the fifth inning and at one point struck out
four future Hall of Famers consecutively—Charlie
Gehringer, Ruth, Lou Gehrig, and Jimmie Foxx.
The only run he allowed was on a home run by
Ruth in the seventh as the Americans won 1 to 0.

Sawamura was on a Japanese team that traveled
to the United States for an exhibition tour, and he
could have been the first Japanese player to play in
the major leagues but he turned down the offer. He
told one U.S. magazine, "My problem is I hate
America and I cannot make myself like Americans."

Sawamura remained in Japan and continued to
pitch brilliantly, one year winning thirty-three
games. He fought in World War II and was killed
when a torpedo sank his ship.

The Japanese talked for years about Ruth's visit
to their country. He had to be guarded every time
he stepped out of the team's hotel, and he was said
to have signed so many autographs he could no
longer write. A crowd of 65,000 showed up for his
first game.

In a luncheon address during the American tour,
Japan's Prince Tokugawa said that more schoolboys in his country knew the names of Babe Ruth
and Connie Mack than could accurately name the
Japan premier.

"It is no longer possible for you Americans to

claim baseball as a national game for America alone," Tokugawa said.

By 1936, Japan's first professional league had been established. Most of the teams were owned either by newspapers, trying to increase circulation, or by railways, hoping to increase travel on their lines. As the game was increasing in popularity, however, war broke out. The game took a backseat to the war effort. Games were suspended so the players could enlist in the military. Stadiums either became ammo dumps or were torn down so the land could be used to grow barley. Beginning in 1935, the Japanese Board of Education prevented schoolboys from playing baseball because of concentration on war calisthentics.

"The Nippon League had similar obstacles during the war as in the United States," *The Sporting News* reported in 1945. "Player shortages at first forced a curtailment of the league to six teams, and finally the abandonment of the loop in 1945. As Sataro Suzuki (a Tokyo sports editor) stated, 'We admired baseball officials and the government in the United States for keeping the game alive during the war. I wish we were as fortunate.' "

During World War II, animosity toward everything American prompted baseball officials in Japan to come up with Japanese words for all of the common terms used during a game, such as strike, ball, pitcher, batter, and base, words that had been left in English until then.

Just as many promising American players went
off to war, never to return, the same was true in
Japan. One such player was Nagoya pitcher Shin-
ichi Ishimaru, who died as a kamikaze pilot while
attacking a U.S. ship in 1944.

About 200 players entered the Japan Army and
Navy, with about 20 reported killed during the war.

After the war, however, the Allies viewed baseball as a way to help rebuild Japan. It was reported
that Allied high command officials allowed the
game to resume, believing it would provide a good
morale boost. Large corporations again stepped up
and agreed to either own or sponsor teams.

In November 1945 a game was played between
Keio and Waseda universities at the Meiji Shrine
Stadium in Tokyo before a large crowd that in-
cluded many American troops.

One of the worries about resuming professional
games in Japan after the war was the food shortage.
League officials said the players would cultivate
their own crops. "Thus, the ballplayers plan to keep
in good health during the winter and will have a
supply of food on hand to carry them through the
1946 championship season," *The Sporting News* reported.

A new baseball stadium was built, home for the
Hiroshima Carp, directly across the street from
where the atomic bomb fell on Hiroshima.

"Out of the ruins of the bomb, one of the first
things they built was a baseball park," Ted Heid,

director of Pacific Rim scouting for the Mariners, told the *Seattle Post-Intelligencer*. "During the Allied occupation, baseball was a big part of that country coming back together. Our armed forces rebuilt fields right away. Our servicemen liked it because they could play, and it was a chance for Americans and Japanese to play against each other."

The Japanese began embracing more and more aspects of American culture, and it was only natural that their love of baseball increased. Baseball quickly became the country's favorite sport. By 1950 the professional league had split into two, the Central and the Pacific, each with six teams, modeling the American and National leagues in the United States.

Major league teams continued to play in Japan on postseason exhibition tours. When a Japanese team actually beat a U.S. squad, which was playing without Joe DiMaggio, in 1951, it touched off a national celebration.

The Yomiuri Giants quickly became the most successful team in Japan, thanks in large measure to their owners, a media conglomerate. Just as television was becoming popular, more Giants games were shown than of any other teams. The *Yomiuri Shimbun* was the most widely read newspaper in the country, and it helped increase the team's popularity.

Sadaharu Oh, perhaps the only Japanese player

known by many Americans, began his professional career with the Giants in 1958. Before retiring twenty-two years later, he hit 868 home runs and led the team to nine consecutive Japanese championships between 1965 and 1973.

The team had the money to buy whatever players it wanted, and before long other teams began complaining about that unfair advantage. To help address the imbalance, a draft was created in 1965, designed to help spread out the talented players so they would not all end up on the Giants.

The power of the Giants was still intense, however. In 1978 the team signed pitcher Suguru Egawa to a contract, even though the college star had been drafted by the Hanshin Tigers. When the baseball commissioner ruled the signing illegal, the Giants threatened to withdraw from the Central League and form a new league. The commissioner backed down and Egawa was allowed to play for the Giants.

The less-successful Pacific League had to look to more innovations and ideas to spur interest and attendance. The league introduced the designated hitter, devised a schedule format where the winner of the first half of the season had a playoff against the second-half winner, and came up with team mascots and neon uniforms. The league even staged one particularly racy advertising campaign featuring players' backsides, aimed at attracting more female fans.

The most successful team to come out of that league was the Seibu Lions, owned by the Seibu Corporation. The Lions won eleven pennants and eight Japan Series titles between 1982 and 1994.

The Japanese knew, from the tours that the U.S. teams had made to Japan, that the Americans were more advanced in their knowledge of baseball skills and fundamentals. That is why several Japanese were thrilled at the opportunity to spend time with American teams during spring training. Four Japanese stars went to camp with the minor league San Francisco Seals in 1951, and two players and the manager of the Tokyo Giants went to camp with the Dodgers in 1957.

The Yankees were the first major league team to hire a scout in Japan, Bozo Wakabayashi, in 1956. Baseball expert Casey Stengel predicted that it would be only a matter of time before a Japanese player made a successful jump to the major leagues.

"It may be four or five years, but I think the next great innovation in American baseball will be a Japanese star," Stengel said in 1956.

Another Japanese visitor in the mid-1950s, Dodger general manager Al Campanis, agreed that a U.S. team would soon be signing players from Japan.

"I was amazed at the ability of these Japanese teams," Campanis said. "We must admit they've made tremendous strides."

Part of the drawbacks of the Japanese player then were similar to what some critics said about the chance for Ichiro be successful with the Mariners in 2001.

In a 1956 story, *The Sporting News* said, "Several drawbacks confront the Japanese who dream of playing in America. The big obstacles are stature and lack of strength to be a consistent, day-after-day major leaguer. Weak arms also are a hindering characteristic found in Japanese performers.

"The contrast between American and Japanese players is sharp because of the vast difference in living and diet conditions between the two countries. Because of the economic situation in Japan, it is difficult, to put it mildly, for a Japanese athlete to progress equally with his American counterpart.

"Also, because of economics, a real baseball is a luxury not enjoyed by many kids. Youngsters play with a light, soft rubber ball until they are fortunate enough to join one of the pro teams, and, by that time, they have lost years of growing up with a standard baseball."

The thing that impressed Campanis the most when he was in Japan was how many youngsters he saw playing baseball. "At any hour of the day you can't go by a piece of open property without seeing some youngsters playing catch or perhaps a little pepper," he said. "One thing I'll never forget was the sight of some youngsters playing on a small lot which had been created by a demolition bomb. Here was a bunch of Japanese kids playing an American game on a field made by an American bomb.

"That proved to me more than anything else that the Japanese people don't resent us. I don't know how you'd find better proof."

As Japanese teams began to look for more and better ways to educate their players, it became increasingly obvious that players should travel to the United States. One team, the Nankai Hawks, decided to send three of its youngest players to spend the 1964 season playing in the minor league organization of the San Francisco Giants. One of the three was Masanori Murakami, a left-handed pitcher. Murakami spent most of 1964 pitching for Class A Fresno, where he helped lead the team to the California League championship. The other two players spent the year in a lower minor league and, not considered prospects, were returned to Japan at the end of the season.

Murakami, however, was very impressive. Despite struggling to understand English, the young man proved quickly that he was able to understand baseball. *The Sporting News* reported that, in Murakami's first game for Fresno, manager Bill Werle summoned him from the bullpen in the ninth inning with Fresno leading 1 to 0, one out and runners on first and second.

Werle pointed to the scoreboard, hoping Murakami understood the game situation. Then he said "low" and twisted his wrist, trying to tell Murakami he wanted him to throw his curve ball, his best pitch. As he turned to go back to the dugout, Murakami said to his manager, "OK to throw double-play ball?"

Werle turned back around and said yes. On the first pitch, the batter grounded into a game-ending double play.

Murakami was just as impressive for the rest of the season, but he still was surprised when he received word that he was being called up by the Giants to the major leagues. That had not been part of the agreement between the Giants and Nankai, at least as far as Murakami knew. Still, he reported and made nine relief appearances for the Giants, posting a 1 and 0 record with a 1.80 earned run average (ERA).

A dispute arose over whether Murakami would be allowed to remain with the Giants in 1965, primarily because the Japanese team had failed to realize, when it had agreed to send the players to the United States and signed away their contracts, that the release gave the Giants permission to call any of those players up to the majors for a fee of only $10,000. Thus, the Giants argued, they now controlled Murakami's rights.

Murakami was under tremendous political and family pressure to remain in Japan, even though he wanted to pitch for the Giants. In January 1965 he wrote to Giants owner Horace Stoneham and said he had decided to remain in Japan.

"I feel," Murakami wrote, "that my place is with my family since I am an only son. I didn't know how much Japan meant to me, but now I have a girl in Osaka and I feel I will be homesick if I leave."

Still, the Giants refused to budge and insisted that Murakami was under contract to them. The commissioners of the two leagues became involved, and at one point Commissioner Ford Frick suspended all negotiations between American and Japanese clubs until Murakami's contract dispute was resolved.

Finally a compromise was reached. Murakami would be allowed to pitch for the Giants again in 1965. Both teams agreed that thereafter he would be free to decide if he wanted to remain in the United States or return to Japan in 1966.

Murakami finally joined the Giants in May of 1965 and had an outstanding year. He pitched in forty-five games, forty-four of them in relief, and was 4 and 1 with a 3.75 ERA. In his two years combined, he struck out a hundred batters in 89⅓ innings and walked only twenty-three.

Murakami quickly became a fan favorite of San Francisco's Japanese community and among his teammates, who told the story of how Murakami went out one day during spring training looking for some souvenirs. When he returned empty-handed, they asked why he had not purchased anything. "No good, no good," Murakami said. "Everything made in Japan."

Murakami also showed his humor and his baseball knowledge when he talked about his pitching, especially as a relief pitcher. "I throw fastball and curve," he said shortly after joining the Giants. "But no change-up. The change-up no good. Relief pitcher come in, men on bases. Throw change. Boom! Long ball. No good."

The Giants wanted to sign Murakami again for 1966, but he gave in to all of the pressures in Japan and returned to his homeland. He pitched in Japan for many years but had only one effective season, going 18 and 4 in 1968.

While Murakami at least tried to move to the United States, other Japanese stars elected to stay home. Although Sadahara Oh was the most widely known Japanese player in the United States, the most popular player in Japan ever was his teammate, Shigeo Nagashima. Nagashima led the league in home runs twice, in RBIs five times, and won six batting titles. Oh and Nagashima batted third and fourth for the Giants until Nagashima retired in 1974. Fittingly, he homered in his final game.

Another Japanese star was Sachio Kinugasa, the son of a U.S. serviceman. He set Japan's consecutive game streak by playing in 2,215 straight games, breaking Lou Gehrig's record before Cal Ripken Jr. did. Kinugasa's streak nearly ended at

1,123 games in 1979, after a pitch fractured his left shoulder. Despite doctor's orders that he sit out, Kinugasa played the following day. He said, "It would have been even more painful for me to stay home."

The best base runner in Japan in that era was Yutaka Fukumoto. His team insured his legs against injury. Fukumoto stole 1,065 bases during his career, a record 106 in 1972, and that total did not include two he stole in an exhibition game with Johnny Bench catching.

Probably the greatest pitcher in Japanese history was Masaichi Kaneda, who won 400 games and struck out 4,490 batters in his career despite playing for the Swallows, a perennially bad team. He lost twenty-three games in his career by the score of 1 to 0.

The only Japanese player to reach the 3,000 hit mark was Isao Harimoto, who was born in Hiroshima and was in his mother's arms outside the city when the atomic bomb exploded. His sister was killed in the blast. He grew up to win seven batting titles in his career.

After Murakami returned to Japan, no other Japanese players made the jump to the United States until 1972, when the Japanese league loaned three players to the Lodi Lions in the Class A California League. The men suffered from severe homesickness, however, and were not able to make a successful transition to the United States.

It was only natural that some U.S. players would wind up playing in Japan. The player generally considered the first American star in Japan was Wally Yonamine, a native of Hawaii, who broke in with the Tokyo Giants in 1951, playing fifty-four games. The outfielder won three batting titles and in 1957 was named the league's Most Valuable Player. Japanese teams tried to lure U.S. players to their country as early as 1952, offering major leaguers a salary of $5,000 plus travel and living expenses.

The now more common practice of U.S. players going to Japan near the end of their careers was unheard of until 1962, when former stars Don Newcombe and Larry Doby moved overseas to the Chunichi Dragons.

What Newcombe, Doby, and all of the other Americans who have left the United States and moved to Japan discovered, however, was that even though they were still playing baseball, the game was quite different.

The regular season in Japan is shorter, 130 games, as opposed to 162 in the United States, but the average day is much longer. While major leaguers in the United States might show up three or four hours before a night game and take some batting practice and fielding practice, the Japanese have long and rigid practices, even on game days.

The Americans found out it is not unusual for a

player's work day to be eight hours long—at a minimum.

Bob Nieman had played in the majors for twelve years before he signed to play in Japan in 1963. He wasn't prepared for the culture shock. "Any American who thinks he's going to Japan to play ball the way we know it is just plain crazy," he said in a 1964 interview. "You wouldn't believe some of the things they do over there."

Nieman was particularly surprised by how much and how seriously the Japanese took their practice sessions. And even though he played there almost forty years ago, the situation is basically the same today.

"The Japanese believe wholeheartedly that practice makes perfect," Nieman said. "So they practice all the time. Spring training begins the first week of January; they open the season about the same time as we do; then at the end of the season they have 'fall' practice. You wind up playing ball eleven months of the year."

Brian Raabe was a longtime minor leaguer in the United States who played seventeen games in the majors before he signed with the Seibu Lions in 1998. "The first day of spring training we started at eight in the morning and ran for forty-five straight minutes. First thing we did. We just ran hard. They believe that once you're tired, then you start to work," he said.

Raabe had heard about how seriously the Japanese took the game, but he wasn't prepared when he actually became a part of it.

"The players there don't enjoy baseball like we do over here," Raabe said. "If you try to have fun and lighten the game up, they don't like that. They're more of a stern face, get the ball and go 'This isn't fun, this is business.' "

He learned that lesson several times over, but one particular day sticks in his mind.

"Our starting pitcher, the ace of the team, got the flu one day and the coach called a team meeting and told us he was fined $1,000 for not being able to pitch," Raabe told the *Seattle Post-Intelligencer*. "When I heard that through the translator, I just started laughing, because I thought he was kidding. But he wasn't kidding."

Steve Ontiveros, a former member of the Chicago Cubs, played in Japan for almost six years and still had a hard time digesting the differences between the two countries' approach to the game.

"I've never seen anything like a Japanese training camp," Ontiveros said. "In the American majors, we were on the field from 10 A.M. until 2 P.M. every day and we were ready to start the season in three weeks. In Japan, we're all out there from January, seven to eight hours a day, with lectures and indoor workouts in the evening. It's incredible."

Matt Stairs played in Japan briefly in 1994 and experienced many of the same problems that Raabe observed.

"If you make a couple of errors, you don't last too long," Stairs said. "They don't take that crap. You make an error or two and you're on the bench. I made an error one game and made an error in the first inning of the next game, and I was out of the game by the second inning. We had one game where we went through four right-fielders."

Tom O'Malley was one of the more successful American players in Japan, and he saw players come and go. The ones who wanted to be there and tried to better themselves during the experience were the ones who lasted the longest and enjoyed the greatest success, he said. O'Malley played six seasons in Japan, winning the league batting title in 1993.

"I was willing to adapt to their culture and their style of play," O'Malley said in a 1997 interview. "You can't go over there and complain. You have to do it their way. You have to be disciplined. They teach you discipline."

Former Dodger Reggie Smith was the first foreign player to sign for $1 million a year in Japan, getting the deal with the Yomiuri Giants in 1983. He showed he was worth the money by hitting twenty-eight homers and leading his team to the pennant. Still, he had provisions in his contract that limited his pregame workouts, provisions that were a source of discontent for many Japanese. One television commentator said that Smith "should take more fielding practice in the interest of team harmony."

American players had to learn the customs of the Japanese game, customs that make it different from the version played in the United States and Canada. Another person who had to make similar adjustments was Bobby Valentine, when he agreed to manage in Japan. Now managing the New York Mets, Valentine is the first person to manage in both leagues.

In Japan, it is not uncommon for games to end between 10:15 and 10:30 P.M., no matter the inning or the score, so fans, stadium workers, and even players can use public transportation to return home. Foul balls hit into the stands have to be returned to the ushers. Pitchers usually don't try to move hitters away from the plate, and takeout slides on the bases and collisions at home plate are very rare. Looking at the scoreboard also can be confusing, because the ball and strike count is reversed, with the number of strikes listed first and then the number of balls. And players have to put up with a very aggressive Japanese media, more intrusive into a player's private life than even reporters in New York.

Knowing what troubles Americans have had in trying to adjust to playing baseball in Japan only increases the respect that Americans have for Japanese who have come over and adjusted well to the U.S. game.

Much like the Spanish-speaking players from the Dominican Republic have found, playing the game is sometimes the easiest adjustment a player has to make. Learning how to get around town, how to order food in a restaurant, and how to make all the day-to-day decisions in a strange country where you don't speak the language is a much more difficult task.

That's exactly what Hideo Nomo found out in 1995 when he became the first Japanese player since Murakami to successfully make the transition from Japan to the majors.

CHAPTER 3

Nomomania

Hideo Nomo's signing with the Los Angeles Dodgers on February 13, 1995, was much bigger news in Japan than it was in Los Angeles. There were fifteen television camera crews and two dozen still photographers at the news conference in a hotel ballroom, most wanting to snap his picture and transmit it back to Japan.

Nomo, whose first name means "hero" in Japanese, had been literally that in his homeland. In his first four professional seasons, he led the Japanese league in victories and strikeouts. He had won at least seventeen games a year in a 130-game season. At the age of twenty-six, he was entering his baseball prime. He was wealthy, earning a salary of $1.5 million a year. He was one of the most recognizable people–not just athletes–in Japan.

Still, in Nomo's mind, something was missing. That something was a challenge, and he considered jumping to the major leagues the greatest possible challenge he could face. It was a decision no one could talk him out of, not his family or close friends. He knew the risk he was taking, he knew the pressure he would be under, he knew what would happen if he failed.

"It's my life, that's the only way I could look at it," Nomo told the *Los Angeles Times*. "I knew what the risks were. I knew everybody was watching. But I also knew that if I didn't do this, I would spend the rest of my life regretting it."

His mind made up, Nomo faced a tougher problem. He had to find a way to get out of his contract with the Kintetsu Buffaloes. In 1995, rules in the Japanese league prevented a player from becoming a free agent until he had played for ten years, and Nomo was still several years away. He hired an agent, Don Nomura, to represent him and to look into his options.

In turn, Nomura hired an agent from the United States, Arn Tellem, to look into Nomo's contract and see if he could find a loophole Nomo could use to get out of the deal. Tellem found it—if Nomo announced his retirement, he could become a free agent. There was no provision against moving to another country and playing if he retired; the contract specified only that he could not move to another team in Japan.

"There were two critical aspects," Tellem has said. "The Japanese had to recognize that the escape provision was legitimate, and the commissioner's office had to accept it and acknowledge that Nomo couldn't be prevented from signing with an American team, although they initially tried to prevent it."

So at the age of twenty-six, Nomo announced

his retirement. Once attorneys for Major League Baseball were convinced Nomo was acting on his own and Kintetsu agreed not to challenge Nomo's departure, it gave its blessing for teams to negotiate with him. One of the first calls Nomura received that day was from the Dodgers, whose president, Peter O'Malley, had been one of the leading proponents of expanding the American game into foreign markets.

Nomura sent a two-minute film clip of his client to all of the major league teams and heard back from many. A trip to the States was scheduled for late January and early February, with the first two stops in Seattle and San Francisco.

The Giants entertained Nomo and Nomura at dinner. Owner Peter Magowan was so interested that he called on the Japanese consulate and Murakami for help in trying to sign Nomo. The Giants were in much the same bind with Nomo as the other clubs were, however: They were working without any real information from scouts who had seen him pitch.

The Nomo-Nomura duo flew south to meet with the Dodgers. More meetings were scheduled with the Yankees, Braves, and Marlins. Nomo threw a few pitches in the Los Angeles bullpen to pitching coach Dave Wallace but couldn't really show his ability because of tendonitis in his right shoulder, which had bothered him during his final 1994 season in Japan.

Even though no one in the organization had seen Nomo pitch except on that two-minute video clip, the Dodgers offered Nomo a rookie-year salary of $109,000 and a $1 million signing bonus. Nomura turned the offer down, saying it wasn't good enough, and prepared to take Nomo on to New York. O'Malley stopped them, coming up with another million to increase the signing bonus to $2 million, and Nomo became a Dodger.

"It shows they [the Dodgers] have more money than us," Giants manager Dusty Baker said at the time. "They can take a chance. This is probably what you call a speculative investment. Wildcatting."

Likely no Dodger executives, scouts, or other personnel would have been willing to predict on that February day in 1995 what Nomo would do in a Los Angeles uniform. There really was no way to know.

"There was just something about him," Dodgers executive vice president Fred Claire told the *Los Angeles Times*. "Here's a guy who had everything in Japan. He had fame, fortune, a good life. He gave it all up just so he could pitch against the best. That impressed us. That impressed us a lot."

Added scouting director Terry Reynolds, "It takes a unique personality with a real desire to come here and play. How often do you see one of our star players in the prime of his career leaving his family and giving up his salary and security to go there?"

Even though he knew he had made the proper decision, Nomo still had trouble sleeping the night before he was to leave Japan and fly to join the Dodgers in spring training in Vero Beach, Florida. He had not enjoyed a great relationship with the press in Japan, mainly because of invasions of his privacy, so he was not surprised that only about a dozen journalists were at the airport to see him off.

The Dodgers were surprised that Nomo did not have a better reputation among the Japanese media, thinking the signing would produce a flood of positive stories and attention for the team in Japan. What was more surprising, however, was that when Nomo reported to Vero Beach, his arm was so sore he could not throw off a mound.

Looking into his pitching records, the Dodgers were shocked to learn that Nomo had thrown more than 140 pitches in a game an astounding sixty-one times. In one game he had been allowed to remain even though he walked sixteen batters and threw 198 pitches. In another game, he had made 191 pitches. In high school, he reportedly went through stretches when he pitched four games in five days.

The team immediately put him on an extensive rehabilitation program, hoping they had not made a bad investment.

Concerned about Nomo's medical condition, Wallace decided to say something to Nomo about the rehabilitation program one day when O'Malley was hosting a pool party for the team. Speaking through an interpreter, Wallace told Nomo, "Listen, Hideo, I want feedback from you as we go along. I want your suggestions. I want your thoughts."

As Nomo listened to the translation, he smiled. Wallace said later, "I have a feeling that kind of conversation doesn't happen much in Japan."

Growing up in Japan, Nomo had operated under the discipline that is the dogma of that country.

Born in Osaka, Nomo was the son of a postman. His father fed him boiled fish paste as a boy in hopes that he would grow up big and strong. Nomo developed into a baseball player at Seijyo High School, graduating in 1986. He became a member of Japan's national team, which won a silver medal at the 1988 Olympics in Seoul, South Korea.

From 1986 through 1989, Nomo played in Japan's Industrial League for Shin-Nitte Tsu, then moved up to the Professional League with the Kintetsu Buffaloes. It was there that he began to receive national attention after posting an 18 and 8 record with a 2.91 ERA, good enough to win the Rookie of the Year and Most Valuable Player awards. He also won the Sawamura Award, which goes to the pitcher of the year.

Nomo also got his first experience against major leaguers from America, pitching three games in relief on a U.S. postseason tour of Japan.

Over the next three years, Nomo proceeded to

win fifty-two games and led the league in strikeouts each season. He reached the 1,000-career strikeout mark faster than any pitcher in Japanese baseball history.

Nomo experienced his first subpar season in 1994, when a shoulder injury limited him to an 8 and 7 record in seventeen starts. It was after that season, when he was locked in a salary dispute, that he demanded to be traded. When the Kintetsu Buffaloes refused that request, Nomo set off on the journey that led him to Los Angeles.

He had grown to 6 foot 2 inches, 210 pounds, and had earned the nickname "the Tornado" because of his unorthodox windup. That motion made it difficult for hitters to pick up the release of the ball. Even if they did see it, Nomo's devastating forkball made him almost unhittable at times.

Even though he had been so successful in Japan, no one could predict what kind of success Nomo would have in the major leagues. He came to spring training with his shoulder still hurting from the year before, and with major leaguers locked out of camp in a labor dispute, evaluating Nomo became even harder. Once the major leaguers reported to Florida and Nomo's shoulder pain subsided, however, the Dodgers began to get a clearer look. More and more they liked what they saw.

After Nomo made one minor league start for Bakersfield in the Class A California League, the Dodgers were ready to see what he could do. On

May 2, 1995, he made his major league debut with a starting assignment against the Giants at Candlestick Park.

Not understanding the depth of the rivalry between the Dodgers and Giants probably was a good thing for Nomo.

"It'd be like me going to a foreign country, hearing them yell stuff at me, and smiling, and I'd smile back," said Dusty Baker.

Added Los Angeles outfielder Chris Gwynn, "He'll be better off than me. I made my first start here, and I felt like I was going to war."

The game was televised live back to Japan, beginning at 4:30 A.M., and was covered by ninety Japanese reporters and twenty-nine news services. Nomo could not have performed much better, pitching five shutout innings and striking out seven. The fact that the Dodgers eventually lost the game, 4 to 3, in fifteen innings mattered to only a few.

After striking out the first batter he faced, Darren Lewis, and getting a ground out, Nomo walked the bases loaded. After pitching coach Dave Wallace made a trip to the mound, Nomo was able to strike out Royce Clayton to end the inning.

The headline on Mike Downey's column in the *Los Angeles Times* the following morning was a question: "The Start of Something Big?" The term "Nomomania" was used in the article, perhaps for the first time.

It would be a month before Nomo would get his

first win, a 2 to 1 victory over the Mets on June 2. Over the next four weeks, however, Nomo took off and captured national attention in two countries, the United States and Japan. On June 14 he struck out sixteen Pirates, setting a Dodger rookie record. By the time he shut out Colorado on June 29, he had won six games in a row with an ERA of 0.98 in that span and become the hottest story in baseball.

He was the National League's pitcher of the month in June. He also became the first rookie pitcher to start the All-Star game since the Dodgers' Fernando Valenzuela in 1981.

In owner Peter O'Malley's office at Dodgers Stadium, there was only one picture of a player— Hideo Nomo.

"Nobody's more excited about what Nomo has accomplished than me," O'Malley told the *Los Angeles Times*. "It's just incredible. I think our fans want to see someone new, someone fresh. They want to be in on the beginning of someone's career. They want to enjoy and savor this moment, just like they did with Fernando.

"In my twenty-five years as club president, Fernandomania was my most exciting period. Well, we're at the threshold of something here."

Not only were Dodger fans excited, everyone in baseball was captivated by Nomo's success. And it came at a critical time for the game which was trying to recover its fans after labor problems the previous year had led to the cancellation of the World Series.

"It's a great story," said catcher Mike Piazza. "I never thought it was going to be this big, this much of a happening. It takes a special kind of guy to deal with all that attention. He's done it extremely well."

Said frequent All-Star Tony Gwynn, "We were watching people following him around for two days. It got to a point where he couldn't even go to the bathroom without people following him. There was a camera crew that literally followed him through the door. Then they realized it was a bathroom and turned around. You should have seen their faces."

Nomo was just as impressive in the All-Star game as he had been in the regular season, pitching two shutout innings. He struck out three of the six hitters he faced and allowed only one hit.

Off the field, his popularity was displayed not once, but twice, with two Nike ads making their debut during the televised game.

Nomo admitted at the game that he also had had some doubts about what level of success he would have in the majors. Those doubts, he said, were now gone.

"Now I think I can do it," he said through an interpreter. "From here on, I think I will be up to the task."

That is indeed what happened. He pitched his

first career one-hitter. He broke the Dodger rookie season strikeout record. He beat the Padres on the next to last day of the regular season to clinch the NL West division title. Nomo finished the year with a 13 and 6 record, a 2.54 ERA, and 236 strike-outs in 191⅓ innings, but statistics alone do not give an accurate description of that season.

"Just when baseball had its problems, here comes this young man from Japan with a unique delivery and great ability," said Los Angeles manager Tommy Lasorda. "All of a sudden, he's got the world chasing him and wanting to see him pitch."

Whereas only a few reporters had gathered at the Osaka airport when Nomo left for spring training in February, a crowd of more than 1,000 was awaiting his arrival in October. His success was voted the sports story of the year in Japan, and he received numerous awards and tributes as he returned a conquering hero.

One of the most unusual came from a high school in the Kouchi Prefecture of Japan, where students collected 20,000 recyclable cans and created a mural of Nomo that was twelve meters wide and fifteen meters high.

On New Year's Eve, many Japanese stayed home to watch a twelve-hour special on Nomo that aired on national television.

It was speculated that Nomo's success would lead to more players from Japan wanting to come to the United States. While some did follow, not as many made the leap as probably had the ability to do so.

"The most significant part is that for 30 years the Japanese didn't know how their players compared to ours," Lasorda told the *Los Angeles Times*. "What he's done has been a big boost to their baseball program."

Nomura, the agent who negotiated Nomo's leap across the Pacific, said he thought that while many Japanese players would like to follow Nomo, the final analysis would keep them in their own country.

"I think most Japanese players would consider the risk and stay in Japan," he told the *Times*. "It's very difficult to throw everything away and start a new life. I also think Nomo made a real history-making move, but the real measure of it is that it should enhance the position of Japanese players. . . . They have been like puppets on a string to the corporations owning the teams. Whether they follow Nomo or use it as leverage, they are now in position to negotiate a better deal."

Nomo didn't really view himself as a pioneer; he was more concerned with repeating, and improving on, the success of his rookie season. He had erased the doubts that he could be an effective pitcher in the major leagues, and he had removed the first-year pressure of knowing he was representing the country of Japan.

"My God, after what he had to go through last year, I think this season will be a lot easier," Lasorda said in spring training of 1996. "Last year, he didn't know what he was going to do. There was always a doubt: 'Can I do it?' He knows he can do it now."

Indeed, his season got off to a roaring start. Nomo threw a shutout in the Dodgers' home opener, and he followed that game with a seventeen-strikeout performance against Florida in his next start.

Nomo saved his best game for September, however, when he went into the hitter's paradise known as Coors Field in Denver and pitched a no-hitter against the Rockies.

Befitting his usual stoic nature, Nomo was about the only person at Coors Field the night of September 17 who wasn't excited. When he made a postgame stop at a convenience store on his way back to the team hotel, he suddenly found himself autographing napkins, sandwich wrappers, anything the customers could stick in front of him.

"I was more excited," said Michael Okumura, Nomo's translator. "It's almost like he had to calm me down.

"Psychologically, spiritually, he wants to be cool. If he gets too excited and says the wrong thing, it would be all over. That's why he's very careful in telling people what he wants to say."

Nomo's teammates also were excited.

"It's the most incredible thing I've ever seen in baseball," reliever Mark Guthrie said. "You'll never see it again. You can sit there and say all the superlatives, but people don't understand what a feat that was."

Nomo ended the year with a 16 and 11 record and became the first Dodger pitcher to strike out more than 200 batters in each of his first two seasons since Don Sutton in 1972–1973.

The following season, even more of the pressure and overwhelming attention had subsided and Nomo settled in as a more-regular starting pitcher. He won fourteen games but lost twelve, and saw his ERA climb to 4.25. He did become the fastest pitcher in major league history to record 500 strikeouts, breaking the mark set by Dwight Gooden. Another highlight came on June 18, in a game against the Angels. Reliever Shigetoshi Hasegawa also pitched in the game, marking the first game in major league history that two Japanese-born players appeared in the same game.

By this time Nomo was having more medical problems, and at the end of the season he underwent surgery to remove calcium deposits near his right elbow.

Just as his arrival and sudden success had been so unexpected, the end of Nomo's career as a Dodger was just as stunning. He was not pitching well, with a 2 and 7 record and 5.05 ERA, prompting him to demand a trade. Before he and Nomura could hold a news conference on June 1 to make that demand public, Fred Claire called both men into his office and told them Nomo was being designated for assignment.

The *Los Angeles Times* reported that Nomo had been fired "like a misbehaving peanut vendor," a dramatic fall from grace.

"It's true that I definitely need a change of scenery, a change of environment," Nomo said that day. "I want to go a team that needs me, that needs my pitching."

O'Malley, who had sold the Dodgers but still maintained an office at the stadium, had a special visitor that day. Nomo presented O'Malley with the ball he had hit for his first career homer earlier in the season—the first homer ever hit in the majors by a Japanese-born player. O'Malley told Nomo that he should give the ball to his son and that he would keep it for him.

"I will continue to be close to him and support him," O'Malley told the *Times*. "He knows he has a good friend here."

One of Nomo's good friends on the field, Mike Piazza, had been traded to the Mets less than three weeks earlier. If Nomo could pick where he most wanted to go, the Mets likely would have been his first choice. And three days later his wish was granted; he and pitcher Brad Clontz were traded to the Mets for pitchers Dave Mlicki and Greg McMichael.

In addition to rejoining Piazza, Nomo was united with another Japanese pitcher, Masato Yoshii, and his former pitching coach, Dave Wallace, who now was a special assistant to Mets general manager Steve Phillips.

The presence of those familiar faces should have made Nomo's transition to the Mets easier, but he continued to struggle as he had in Los Angeles. He made sixteen starts and won only four games. Still, the Mets were willing to give him the benefit of the doubt and brought him to spring training in 1999 hoping he would become a regular part of their starting rotation.

He failed to regain the velocity on his fastball and struggled with his control, however, and on March 26 he was placed on waivers.

"We feel like we failed," Wallace told the *New York Daily News*.

For the second time in a year, Nomo was facing an uncertain future. He had to wait two days before agreeing to a minor league contract with the Chicago Cubs. Nomura said he received five other offers but chose the Cubs because they agreed to give him a chance at Triple A Iowa and, after three starts, would either promote him to the majors or release him.

In his third start for the minor league team, Nomo walked six batters in six innings. When the Cubs asked that their agreement be extended so

Nomo could make two more starts at Iowa, Nomura refused, and Nomo was released again.

This time he went to Milwaukee, where suddenly the magic returned. Nomo made one start in
the minors, for Double A Huntsville, where he
struck out seven and pitched seven shutout innings.
Promoted to Milwaukee, he won his debut against
the Giants, allowing one run and five hits in 6⅓
innings.

Nomo went on to win five consecutive games
and finished the year as the Brewers' winningest
pitcher with twelve victories and led the team in
strikeouts.

The 2000 season meant another change of address, and change of leagues, for Nomo. He followed his manager with the Brewers, Phil Garner,
to Detroit, where he became the first Japanese
pitcher to start on opening day, defeating Oakland
7 to 4.

He remained in the Tigers' rotation for the entire
season but struggled to an 8 and 12 record despite
leading the Detroit staff in strikeouts with 181, his
most since 1997. A free agent once more, Nomo
packed up and headed to Boston for the 2001
season.

As the season began, there was little reason to
believe that Nomo, now thirty-two, would perform
any differently than he had for the previous couple
of seasons. The Red Sox were counting on him to
be one of the pitchers in their rotation, but nobody

looked to him to challenge staff ace Pedro Martinez.

Yet in his first start of the season on April 4, Nomo threw another no-no, pitching his second career no-hitter, a 3 to 0 victory over the Baltimore Orioles.

Nomo became only the fourth pitcher in major league history to pitch a no-hitter in each league. The gem was preserved in the ninth inning by second baseman Mike Lansing, who made a backhanded, tumbling catch of a soft liner behind second base hit by Mike Bordick.

Nomo walked three and struck out eleven in pitching the first no-hitter in the ten-year history of Camden Yards.

"I felt pretty good throughout the game," Nomo said through an interpreter. "As I was going into the ninth inning, I was not nervous."

It was the first no-hitter by a Red Sox pitcher since Dave Morehead in 1965, and it allowed Nomo to join Hall of Famers Cy Young, Jim Bunning, and Nolan Ryan as the only pitchers to throw a no-hitter in each league.

The game was televised live in Japan and highlights aired repeatedly in later news shows. One popular sports newspaper printed extra editions, and the game was on the front page of all other major evening newspapers.

One scout who was at the game was Matt Keough, a former pitcher now working for the

Tampa Bay Devil Rays. Watching the game, Keough recalled the first time he had faced Nomo, in a spring training game in Japan when Keough was pitching in that country.

He knew Nomo wasn't throwing as hard on this night as he had years ago, but he also was a better pitcher, Keough told the *Boston Globe*.

"He was facing a good ball club, a good strike zone and a nice cool night to do it on," Keough said. "To his credit, he took advantage of all those things."

Just twenty-two days later, Nomo again flirted with a no-hitter, this time against the Minnesota Twins. He blanked them until Torii Hunter singled leading off the seventh.

Much as in his no-hitter, it didn't dawn on many of the people at the game, including Red Sox pitching coach Joe Kerrigan, for several innings that Nomo was working on a no-hitter. He walked three batters in the first three innings, including the first two batters he faced.

"He was picking up steam as the game wore on," Kerrigan said. "Just like in Baltimore. That splitter is tough to pick up, especially when he has a good feel for it, and he had it tonight. That's when he gets on a roll, when he has a lot of confidence and throws it exactly where he wants it.

"It starts out as a strike, then dips out of the hitter's zone. You could tell the pitch was devas-

tating, just by some of the swings they were taking."

Many in the stands hoped that Hunter's sinking
line drive, which bounced off the glove of right
fielder Darren Lewis, would be called an error, but
it was quickly called a hit. Kerrigan and Nomo,
who turned the game over to the bullpen after the
seventh inning, agreed with the call.

Perhaps Nomo's biggest start of the season, or
at least the most anticipated, was his matchup
against Ichiro in Seattle on May 2.

It was the first time they had faced each other
in four years. On that occasion, in 1997, Nomo was
part of a postseason U.S. delegation to Japan, and
Ichiro greeted him with a single up the middle. The
first time they faced each other, in 1993, Nomo
struck him out. In 1994 Ichiro hit his first Japan
League home run off Nomo.

"I don't think we are bad friends," Nomo said,
"but it's kind of hard to say we're good buddies."

In his first two at-bats, Ichiro grounded out and
flied out. When he came up again in the fifth, a
fastball from Nomo sailed inside and struck Ichiro
in the middle of his back.

"I wanted to throw the pitch inside, but it caught
my finger and it went inside more than I wanted it
to," Nomo said through an interpreter.

The confrontation could have sparked an international incident, but it turned out to be front-page
news only in Japan. Ichiro's comments after the

game showed just how far Japanese players have come in the United States.

"I see him only as one of the opponents," Ichiro said. "And I think he looks at me the same way."

On May 25 Nomo's opponents were the Toronto Blue Jays, and this time his control was perfect. Nomo pitched a one-hitter, struck out fourteen, and didn't walk a batter in pitching the Red Sox to a 4 to 0 victory. The only hit was a double by Shannon Stewart leading off the fourth inning.

No Red Sox pitcher in the last fifty years had pitched a no-hitter and a one-hitter in the same season, and manager Jimmy Williams went so far as to say that he thought Nomo pitched better in the one-hitter.

Going into the game, Nomo had been tied for the league lead in walks with thirty-one. Afterward, Kerrigan recalled a conversation he had had with Nomo a week earlier.

"He said he wanted to pitch more innings, he asked us how he could do it, and we said, 'Well, if you walk less people, you're going to pitch more innings,' " Kerrigan said. "And he said, 'OK, I'm not going to walk anybody.' He's great, he's a man of his word."

Nomo remembered the conversation as well.

"They have to change pitchers when I give up a lot of walks," Nomo said through his interpreter. "I do not want to walk anybody so I can stay in the game."

At one point Nomo struck out seven Toronto batters in a row, one shy of tying the American League record. He retired the last nineteen Blue Jays in order.

"I was just lucky," Nomo said.

Added Kerrigan, "He's a perfectionist. That's the kind of man he is. The guy's looking to better himself even during the game."

It was that desire to better himself and to pitch against the best that led Nomo to make the jump from Japan to the major leagues in 1995. Six years later that same desire was still evident.

"In Japan, I had many issues, here there is an atmosphere of just playing baseball," Nomo told the *Boston Globe* through his interpreter. "You had to set your mind and accept that if you did not succeed, you could not go back and play there again. It was my dream to come here and compete on a higher level, to challenge the best players in the world."

It was because of Nomo's dream, and his success, that the door to the major leagues opened for other Japanese players. Players such as Ichiro and the other Japanese star on the Mariners, reliever Kazuhiro Sasaki, are extremely grateful.

CHAPTER 4

Sasaki

Even before Hideo Nomo decided to challenge Japan's rules and cross the Pacific Ocean to pitch in the major leagues, Kazuhiro Sasaki wanted to do the same thing.

He was pitching for the Yokahama Bay Stars and developing into the best relief pitcher in Japanese baseball history. Like Nomo and other Japanese players who have since come to the majors, he wanted more of a challenge and thought the only place he was going to get it was in the major leagues.

"It was always his dream to come and play in the United States," said Allen Turner, Sasaki's personal interpreter with the Mariners. "He has always said the reason why he came wasn't because Nomo had come and made it easier. He had to wait until he could become a free agent and then he could come."

Unlike Nomo, who found a loophole that allowed him to escape Japan before he was eligible for free agency, Sasaki decided to follow Japan's rules and wait the required ten years before he was granted free agency. The rule has since been

changed to nine years, and teams are learning—as
they did in the United States—that it might be better to move a player before he reaches that mile-
stone if they hope to receive anything of value in
return.

The system in Japan is called "posting," and it
entails listing players whom a Japanese team would
consider allowing to change teams, for a certain
price. Once a player is posted, the team takes bids.
If it receives the price that it is looking for, that
player is allowed to leave and is granted his release.

Part of Sasaki's problem in deciding when to try
to leave Japan was caused by the Yankees' botched
attempt to sign Hideki Irabu from the Chiba Lotte
Marines, even though the San Diego Padres was
the U.S. team that held his rights. The Yankees
finally did acquire Irabu, after making a trade with
San Diego, but the powers in major league baseball
were worried about its relationship with its Japanese brethren and tried to encourage teams to stay
away from Japan until the controversy died down.
Irabu, like Nomo, had not been eligible for free
agency; unlike Nomo, he had not been granted his
release.

Being a good soldier, Sasaki waited his turn,
which only increased his popularity among the Japanese, both while he was still pitching in his homeland and after he signed with the Mariners.

"Sasaki is special in the hearts of the Japanese,"
Florangela Davila wrote in the *Seattle Times* on

April 8, 2001. "They know he's a fighter, how he played 10 years for the Bay Stars, took them to the Japan series championship, had elbow surgery and then took on the marvelous challenge of playing in the United States. They know he isn't a traitor to the Japanese game or its fans because, they say, Sasaki was only ambitious to prove himself against the world's best. His departure wasn't motivated by greed, a characterization radically different than those carried in some media reports a few years earlier about Japanese pitcher Hideki Irabu's signing with the New York Yankees."

What many people, in Japan and the United States, don't know, is that Sasaki was quite often sick as a young boy and that his parents were worried about his health. Frail and prone to high fevers, he spent a lot of time in the hospital. His father, Tadao Sasaki, worked at a milk company and made sure his young son drank milk every day.

On nice days when Kazuhiro was feeling well, father and son would go outside and play catch. The elder Sasaki was a huge baseball fan, who often umpired local games in the Sendai area and managed recreational teams. When Kazuhiro was in the fourth grade, his teacher asked all of the students to write down what they thought their occupation was going to be when they grew up. Like many of the boys, Kazuhiro answered "baseball player."

He went to Tohoku High School, a private

school known for its athletics. People there remember Kazuhiro not only for his baseball ability but because of his other skills. He was known for bringing home stray animals to be nursed. He was said to be a good-natured kid, never complaining, who was honest, kind, patient, someone who worked hard and never gave up.

In high school, Kazuhiro often practiced baseball four or five hours a day. What is perhaps ironic, however, is that while he was earning praise from all of those around him for what kind of young man he was, he became a successful pitcher only because he broke the rules and went behind the back of his coach, Toshiaki Takeda, to learn how to throw a forkball.

The pitch became nearly unhittable in Japan and has been one of the biggest reasons for Sasaki's success in the major leagues.

After high school, Sasaki was able to perfect his specialty pitch further at Tohoku Fukushi University. He then became a first-round pick by Yokohama in the Japanese draft in November 1989 and began his professional career the following spring.

Sasaki appeared in only sixteen games as a rookie, earning two saves, before bursting onto the scene in 1991 with seventeen saves and 137 strikeouts in 117 innings. He was even more dominating in 1992, as he earned twenty-one saves to go with twelve victories. In 87⅔ innings he struck out 135 batters, was selected for the All-Star team for the first time, and also earned his first Fireman of the Year award.

"He was nearly unhittable," said Jim Colborn, now the pitching coach of the Dodgers and formerly the Mariners' director of Pacific Rim scouting. "Yokohama's games were really only eight-inning games because no one could touch him in the ninth. He had tremendous poise and charisma on the mound."

Those factors, plus the fact that at 6 foot 4 inches tall and weighing 200 pounds, he was bigger and more physically intimidating than many Japanese. That only increased the attention he received.

Sasaki even was given a nickname—Daimajin. That was the name of a ferocious deity popularized in a 1966 Japanese fantasy film. In the movie, a spirit enters a stone statue, brings it to life, and then goes off to rescue a village from bad guys, thus earning a "save."

Sasaki earned his second Fireman of the Year award in 1995, when he was 7 and 2 with a 1.75 ERA and saved thirty-two games in forty-seven appearances. He was only warming up.

In 1997 Sasaki was 3 and 0 with a 0.90 ERA and earned thirty-eight saves in forty-nine appearances. The following year, 1998, he set Japanese baseball records with forty-five saves, twenty-two of them coming consecutively. He had an ERA of 0.64 and struck out seventy-eight batters in fifty-six innings.

He followed up that regular season performance by pitching Yokohama to the Japan Series championship. He was named the Central League's MVP and the Pitcher of the Year.

Americans who were on Sasaki's team or playing against him knew his ability rivaled that of the best relief pitchers in the major leagues, and told him so.

Pat Mahomes was his teammate in Yokohama in 1997 and 1998. The two became close friends as Sasaki took Mahomes under his wing and helped with the adjustments the American had to make to living in Japan. He even tried to teach him his forkball.

"I used to mess with him all the time about going over, and he said that when he got enough time in he'd definitely go across," Mahomes said. "The shame about it is, they have to play so long over there, nine years, before they can become a free agent. You still get to see him, but you don't get to see him when he's at his best."

Jeff Manto has bounced around the majors and minor leagues in the United States for years and spent part of the 1996 season in Japan with the Yomiuri Giants. He considers Sasaki the most dominant pitcher he has ever faced.

"I hate to say it, but I felt completely overmatched against him," Manto told the *Seattle Times*. "I've never walked up to the plate saying, 'OK, how many pitches is this going to take?'

"He'd throw exactly what you were looking for

and you still couldn't hit it. He's just filthy. He throws 95, 96 mph with a split-finger pitch that the TV guys call a curveball.

"I remember one game I was the fourth hitter in the inning. He struck out the first three, and I was thankful. If I ever got a hit off him, I would have asked for the ball."

Sasaki stayed in Yokohama in 1999 and suffered through an injury-plagued season. He earned nineteen saves in twenty-three appearances before his season ended on August 9, when he underwent surgery to remove bone chips from his right elbow and to transpose his ulner nerve to ease stress on the joint.

Sasaki was by now one of the most recognizable people in the country. He was the highest-paid player in the Japan League, and he was featured in advertisements for noodles, a vitamin beverage, insurance, the city of Yokohama, and Kirin beer.

What he didn't have, and had been seeking, was that challenge of seeing how successful he could be pitching in the major leagues. Then thirty-one, and with his thirty-second birthday coming up in February before the start of the next season, he knew it was his time to find out.

"In Japan, I had won a championship and had accomplished everything I had looked forward to with my team," Sasaki said. "I wanted to come here and challenge the best, to grow and become a better pitcher."

Sasaki only had two problems—he was still suffering from a tender elbow, which limited the type of workouts he would be able to have, and he didn't know what team he was going to play for.

He hired an American agent, Tony Attanasio, who also was the agent for Mets' manager Bobby Valentine, who had previously managed against Sasaki in Japan. Attanasio arranged a tour for Sasaki to visit with four teams, the Yankees, Mets, Diamondbacks, and Mariners, in mid-November.

Because he was still coming back from the elbow surgery, Sasaki was not able to do more than throw lightly for the different team officials and show them the X rays of his elbow. That combination forced some teams out of the running, including the Mets. They were reluctant to make a multimillion-dollar offer on what some considered a risky signing.

"We are confident he is well on his way back to health," said Mets' general manager Steve Phillips. "His arm is working. He's not cutting himself short with his arm action and delivery, but we weren't looking to try to get him to air out and show us his full velocity."

Still, despite the light workout, Phillips was confident that Sasaki could be a successful pitcher in the major leagues. "The level of dominance may be something you have to consider, but I think there's no question that pitchers who are successful there [in Japan] can have a certain level of success here in the States."

After a stop in Phoenix to see the Diamondbacks, it was on to Seattle, with numerous Japanese reporters in tow. The Mariners, who are owned by Hiroshi Yamauchi, also the owner of Nintendo, rolled out the red carpet. Sasaki stayed at the Four Seasons and received a deluxe tour of the city, including its large Japanese community.

When he arrived at Safeco Field for his light workout, he found uniform number 22 hanging in a locker with his name on the back. That has always been Sasaki's number, in recognition of the fact that he was born in 1968 on February 22 (2–22) at 2:22 A.M.

The locker where the Sasaki jersey was hanging had formerly been the locker of Ken Griffey Jr. Was the implication that the team was making the transition from one savior to the next?

When Sasaki walked out of the dugout and onto the field, the Mariners had arranged for him to be introduced over the loudspeakers as if he were coming into a game: "Now pitching for Seattle, number 22, Kazuhiro Sasaki."

There was a mock line score on the scoreboard, showing the Mariners leading the Yankees 2 to 1 going into the ninth inning. After Sasaki finished throwing, the scoreboard flashed the news that he had done his job, saving a Mariners' fictional victory.

During discussions Sasaki revealed that he had actually been in Seattle before, during a tour while he was in college. Mariners' officials came away from his visit believing they had a good chance of signing him but not wanting to be overconfident.

Sasaki returned to Japan, and was scheduled to come back to the United States in December to visit with additional clubs. However, the Mariners made sure that trip never came off. Working in Japan, the Mariners were able to sign Sasaki to a two-year contract.

They announced the signing in Kyoto, Japan, and the occasion was marked by Yamauchi's first public appearance on Mariners' business.

The Mariners made no promises to Sasaki about his role on the team. Manager Lou Piniella said he expected to go to training camp with incumbent José Mesa installed as the team's closer and Sasaki being used in a setup role. Despite the Mariners' low-key approach to the addition of Sasaki, the news of his signing set off a media frenzy in Japan.

Although the announcement was supposed to be kept secret, more than fifty reporters and cameramen were at the Tokyo airport waiting for Sasaki. During the two-hour limousine ride to Kyoto, a caravan of reporters tried to follow him, resembling a chase scene in an action movie.

"It was stupid," said Colborn, who was traveling with Sasaki. "We tried to lose them like Princess

Di. I thought we were going to run off the freeway and become another story."

"They tried phoning reporters on their cell phones to ask them to back off," the *Seattle Times* reported. "Only a few complied. They phoned the taxi that was trailing behind carrying their luggage and had it stop on a narrow street to block the path of the media cars. It didn't work. As the limo neared the hotel in Kyoto, Sasaki jumped out of the car and into the taxi to whisk him off to a secret location. Fifteen reporters were waiting in the lobby."

Colborn had no doubts about how successful Sasaki could be with the Mariners, but he knew the pitcher also was headed for a change in culture and from the lifestyle he had been used to in Japan.

"He's one of the top five stars in Japan," Colborn told the *Seattle Times*. "If you named our top five guys and think of the lifestyle they have and what their expectations are, and then to go somewhere else where it isn't necessarily going to be that way, and how they'd adjust to that, you'd better have a good stockpile of humility. I hope Sasaki understands that."

Sasaki became the tenth Japanese player, all pitchers, to make the jump to the major leagues.

"Each one becomes a test," Colborn said. "I guess the difference between Sasaki and all the other guys is there will be greater expectations with Sasaki, except for maybe Irabu. All the others were expected to be either role pitchers or fit in. He's going after the stopper role. That's big expectations."

The pressure was coming not only from Sasaki himself but from the Japanese media and the American fans and media. The Mariners had to prepare for a surge in interest in their team, not only from the media trying to cover Sasaki but also from local fans and those in Japan. The team set up a special telephone hot line to provide information in Japanese and announced that sections of the team's website would be translated into Japanese.

Still, when Sasaki actually stepped on the field for the first time in a Mariners uniform at spring training in Peoria, Arizona, the excitement was unbelievable.

Sasaki went into camp saying all of the right things, about how he was a rookie just trying to fit in, but it was clear from the first day of camp that he wanted to become the team's closer, the role he had filled so effectively in Japan for a decade. After all, Mesa wasn't exactly an All-Star in 1999, posting a 4.98 ERA and allowing 124 base runners in only 68⅔ innings.

Going in to camp, Sasaki said that one of his primary goals was to "get the trust of the players, and get in closing situations."

What he also had to get used to was the intense coverage by the Japanese media. On that first day of camp in February, when practice consists of some fielding drills, running, and throwing medium-speed fastballs in the bullpen, twenty Japanese reporters and photographers and three television stations were on hand to cover all of Sasaki's activity. Afterward, he compared the workout to practice in Japan.

"Everything went so fast today," Sasaki said through his interpreter. "In the routine in Japan, you finish one part of the workout, you change shirt, you get time to recover. Here it was rushed. There was not even time to be nervous."

One other difference was when Sasaki discovered that he was scheduled to throw every other day, not the customary every day he had been used to in Japan. He asked the Mariners if he could continue to throw every day and they agreed, as long as he closely monitored the number of pitches he threw each day.

It quickly became obvious that Sasaki was happy with his decision to join the Mariners and that he enjoyed himself when he was pitching. He showed that he was more emotional when he pitched than many of his fellow countrymen, and that was fine with his new teammates and the Mariners' officials.

"There's something about a guy enjoying himself on the field that gives you the sense he's under control," pitching coach Bryan Price said that spring. "The fact that this guy, under the duress and pressure he's facing, can still smile and laugh at himself tells a lot about him."

Sasaki said there was no reason for him not to be having fun, and he praised his new teammates for helping make the transition so easy for him.

"I'm doing something I love to do," Sasaki said through his interpreter. "Of course you have to enjoy that. I don't want to have it be a dreadful experience. I want to have fun while I do my job."

Sasaki also became comfortable giving daily briefings to all of the Japanese reporters covering him, even if he did not contribute in any way to the game that day.

"What he told me is that he wants a good relationship with the Japanese press," Turner said. "He feels that that's the only way for his Japanese fans to learn about his performance. He wants good things written about him. He's just genuinely a friendly guy. He's become like one of my buddies from high school."

Turner came to be associated with the Mariners and Sasaki because of Ted Heid, the Mariners' director of Pacific Rim scouting. "He knew my father through golf," Turner said. "He knew I could do something like this."

Turner was born in California but grew up in Japan, moving to Arizona when he was ten years old. An All-State shortstop in high school, Turner gave up baseball to attend college at Brigham

Young. He returned to Japan on a missionary tour when he was nineteen.

Turner, whose father manages several professional golfers from Japan, majored in Japanese in college. When Heid called and offered him the chance to work as Sasaki's interpreter, he quickly said yes.

The Mariners also tried to make special accommodations for Sasaki by hiring his trainer from Japan, Kiyoshi Egawa, and adding him to the team's training staff.

Hasegawa was another former Japanese pitcher who caught up with Sasaki during the spring, and he offered Sasaki some advice while predicting that he would be successful with the Mariners.

"He can't forget the American hitters have more power," Hasegawa said. "We miss our control sometimes in the middle of the plate, and that means the ball is gone. Don't worry about it. He has to make the same pitches he did in Japan. The first year I came over here, I gave up a lot of home runs, and I got mad. The second year I figured it out.

"In Japan, he was a big star, and he can pitch here too. My best advice—just don't think about it too much."

What Sasaki had to think about in addition to his pitching was all of the other adjustments to moving to a foreign country. Shopping was something he wasn't used to.

"It may not seem like much, but it's very hard to find clothes that fit me in Japan," Sasaki said. "You can't find XXL over there. . . . It's fun for me to come here and be able to find clothes, lots of clothes. It's cost me a lot of money, but there are so many more options."

Sasaki also learned the hard way that he needed to be home to accept an overnight courier delivery. The package contained, among other things, his workout clothes. When he wasn't home, the driver left a note on the door. When he had Turner call about making another delivery, it didn't happen.

"In Japan, if you miss out on a package, you call them and they come right back out that day," Sasaki said. "Maybe the biggest surprise since being here was finding out they don't do that."

Sasaki and the Mariners also discovered that spring that he could be just as effective, and his forkball just as dominating, as had been the case in Japan. In nine appearances covering ten innings, Sasaki allowed only six hits, struck out thirteen and walked only two. When the Mariners set their opening-day roster and prepared to begin the regular season, they had a new closer in the bullpen—Sasaki.

"You can see why he was so dominating," Price said near the end of spring training. "But out of respect for the players here, he's still going to have to show he can get them out day in and day out."

Piniella also was pleased by what he saw in the

spring and had no doubts about handing Sasaki the ball in the closer's role.

"He's fit in very well," Piniella said. "He's a hardworking guy, but he has fun. He has that very relaxed, comfortable demeanor on the mound. The fans in Seattle are going to enjoy watching him. We feel he's going to be a major contributor. He's got experience, he throws strikes and he has that split-finger [fastball]. It's a strikeout pitch."

On the second day of the season, April 5, Sasaki made his major league debut, pitching a scoreless ninth inning against the Red Sox in a game the Mariners won 9 to 3. His first save came the following night, when he struck out the side in the ninth to preserve a 5 to 2 win over Boston.

Sasaski's presence was felt at the box office, as many Japanese natives living in the Seattle area began to attend Mariners' games. At a time when the club was still trying to adjust to the departures of Randy Johnson and Griffey, the addition of Sasaki was giving people a reason to come to Safeco Field.

When Sasaki had signed with the Mariners, the Japanese American Chamber of Commerce quickly organized a welcome-to-town party for him. Five hundred tickets were sold at $10 each, and when Sasaki showed up for the party, the crowd went wild. Fan mail from Japan began arriving in the Mariners' clubhouse, and hits from that country on the team's website began increasing.

In his first month in the majors, Sasaki saved three games. He was getting to know his teammates, and all aspects of his game were positive.

"He's fit in great here," said outfielder Jay Buhner, who was one of those helping Sasaki learn some new English words. "I think that's the way he was over there [in Japan] too, a little off-the-wall kind of crazy Japanese guy. He likes to have a good time, be part of the guys, go out and have a beer or two with us. He's been a nice addition to the ballclub, no doubt."

Added catcher Dan Wilson, "I think he's having a lot of fun. He's always smiling and joking."

Sasaki knew his transition to the majors would not be all fun and games, however, and he hit his first rough spot in May. How he overcame it convinced Piniella, his teammates, and others that he was going to be OK.

In a three-game span, Sasaki allowed two game-ending home runs, unable to save a Seattle lead, and Piniella announced that Sasaki had lost his job as the closer. The manager said he would now use a closer by committee, going with whoever he thought had the best chance of saving the game.

"Sasaki just isn't sharp," Piniella said after Matt Stairs's three-run homer in the May 12 game turned a 7 to 6 Seattle lead into a 9 to 7 loss. "We just can't use him that way anymore. We'll figure it out from here on. We'll get it done somehow."

The biggest concern to the Mariners was why

Sasaki had blown the saves, and the best conclusion was that he was suffering from a sore arm, which he had not mentioned to anybody. Readings on the radar gun showed he had lost three to four miles an hour on his fastball since the start of the season.

Sasaki said he thought the problem was a sore back, the result of sleeping on a soft hotel bed. He insisted there was nothing wrong with his arm.

He got in some extra work with Price in the bullpen. After one game that Mesa saved, the next time the Mariners were in a save situation in the ninth, Sasaki got the ball and came through. He saved two more games in May and began to warm up from that point on, saving eight games in June and ten in July, both tops in the American League.

The key to his success might have been getting better command of his fastball, to go along with his dominating forkball, Price said.

"He has a great forkball, as good as there is, but success is based on the command and quality of his fastball," Price said. "Trusting your stuff is probably the most important thing you can do. The teams that came in to watch us play, they're seeing a closer come in and get outs with his fastball. You have to respect that fastball."

Sasaki believed his improvement was a natural progression and marked his full recovery from his elbow surgery of the previous year.

"They told me at the one-year point it would get

much better and it has," he said in July, eleven months after the operation. "I threw once in Japan after the surgery and I feel far better now than then, or even earlier this season."

Between June 20 and July 28, Sasaki converted fifteen consecutive save opportunities, a Mariners' team record.

"There was some disappointment in May, and he just rediscovered what made him successful in Japan," Price said. "He is the one who had to make the biggest adjustment, both in terms of batters and just being in a new place. I tip my cap to him for doing it."

Sasaki said it did take him some time to learn the differences between baseball in Japan and in the major leagues, even though he had been told what to expect.

"The main difference is the power of the hitters," he told the *Japan Times* through his interpreter, Allen Turner. "Maybe in Japan you would try to keep a one-run lead and focus on defense. Offense is bigger here, and you're always thinking about getting way more than one run.

"Another difference is when we lose a game, the locker room is just silent. Everybody is very down, whereas in Japan after you lose a game, they say, 'Oh well, let's get them tomorrow,' that type of attitude. That's a big difference."

Buhner for one was not surprised at Sasaki's quick success.

"He's picked everything up quick," Buhner said. "He's stepped in and made an immediate impact and he's done a hell of a job closing out games for us. I mean, that's got to be tough. I could never picture myself immediately coming in right away and being 'the guy,' 'the go-to guy.' "

Sasaki saved five games in August, and when he recorded his thirty-second save on September 5, it increased the Mariners' division lead to two and a half games over Oakland. The save also set an American League rookie record, breaking the mark of thirty-one saves set by Billy Koch of Toronto in 1999.

"This was a fresh start for me," Sasaki said. "But as people have asked me about it [the AL record] recently, I did not know of it. I think the pressure of helping the team win has helped me get the record. It is good pressure."

Save number 34 on September 20 in Tampa broke the Mariners' club record for most saves in a season. Sasaki's final save of the season, number 37, came on the last day of the year at Anaheim and clinched the Mariners' appearance in the playoffs as the AL's wildcard team.

The save also broke the major league record for saves by a rookie, which had been thirty-six, set by the Cardinals' Todd Worrell in 1986. Sasaki had only three blown saves for the season, leading the league with a .919 save percentage.

The key to his success was a combination of the

wicked forkball, the redevelopment of his fastball after the elbow surgery, and the ability to make all of the intangible adjustments to living in the United States after spending the first thirty-one years of his life in Japan.

Hitters agreed that the forkball was almost un-hittable at times.

"It drops like a big overhand curveball, the big yellow hammers like Bert Blyleven threw, and Aaron Sele, but it's harder," Buhner said. "I couldn't tell you how many times people have gone and asked the umpire to check the ball, just wondering what the hell the pitch was."

Added catcher Joe Oliver, "Hitters are always making comments how nasty it is, and that's the biggest compliment you can get."

Sasaki just happened to be a guy who developed a proper feel for the pitch, with the proper grip, something that many pitchers try but are not able to master.

"There's guys that throw the fastball faster than me, tons of guys," he said. "The only thing I feel I can beat people on is the forkball. No one can throw that forkball better, so it is a very important pitch for me."

Looking back on his season, Sasaki realized how important it was that he went through a tough time in May and had to learn to pitch his way out of trouble.

"If everything went smoothly, you wouldn't be

able to grow and do well," Sasaki told the *Seattle Times*. "When that happened, I wanted to move forward and I really grew from that. It was definitely a strengthening experience.

"I definitely worried that maybe I don't have good enough stuff to be able to compete here. But I realized, 'It's not going to do any good thinking that.' I'm here, I have to keep competing."

Said Price, "He learned that the way he pitched was enough to be successful in this league. It was trust, trust in his ability. He really started to get on a roll in June and he was a guy comfortable in his environment.

"He probably knew he could fill a role in the majors, but it's different than being the closer where the team's overall success is dependent on you."

Sasaki also was able to overcome the withering media pressure, especially from Japanese reporters who were constantly requesting interviews and information, even on days he didn't pitch.

Even the nonmedia mob of Japanese took special notice of Sasaki every time they saw him.

"In June, we were in a hotel lobby in San Francisco, hanging out and getting ready to go eat dinner," Buhner recalled. "There were probably 100 ladies from Japan, people from a tour, in the lobby at the same time, and in walks Kazu.

"All of a sudden everyone is going 'Sasaki-san.' He took pictures with about three people, then the whole group starting swarming him. His agent had to hurry him out the door before things got out of control."

One of the best pieces of advice Sasaki received during the year came in a telephone conversation with his high school coach, Toshiaki Takeda, during his low period in May.

The advice was simple and straightforward. "He told me not to think about it too much, just go ahead and pitch," Sasaki said.

Sasaki was ready to enter the playoffs keeping that philosophy and approach very much in mind. It was another new experience, and he was determined to do his best.

The Mariners' first-round opponent was the Chicago White Sox, who had finished the regular season with the best record in the American League. Sasaki entered the playoffs on a high note, having allowed only two runs in his last twenty-one innings of work.

There was no change against the White Sox. In saving the first two games of the series in Chicago, Sasaki allowed only one hit and struck out five in his two innings of work.

Still, it might have been difficult for Sasaki to understand exactly what was going on. On the off day before the series resumed in Seattle, Sasaki was in the clubhouse as attendants prepared sheets of plastic to cover the lockers, just in case the Mariners picked up the clinching victory.

Sasaki asked others in the room what was going on. When he was told, Sasaki said, "That's what the plastic is for? We celebrate if we win this round?"

Pitcher Brett Tomko told him, "We celebrate after every round, Kazu. I'm dousing you first."

Indeed, after the Mariners' win the next night completed the three-game series sweep, Sasaki was in front of his locker, joining his teammates in the beer and champagne celebration. "I'm happier than I ever was in Japan," he said.

The victory put the Mariners in the American League Championship Series for the first time since 1995, playing the Yankees.

Sasaki kept his string of impressive performances going in game 1, saving the 2 to 0 victory at Yankee Stadium by pitching a scoreless ninth. Unfortunately for Seattle, the Yankees responded by winning three straight to take a commanding three-games-to-one lead. The Mariners showed life by winning game 5, but the Yankees came back to clinch the AL pennant and a spot in the World Series with a 9 to 7 win in game 6.

Despite their disappointment in not winning the pennant, most people in Seattle had to be pleased with how far the team had come. The season had begun with worries about how the team was going to replace Randy Johnson and Ken Griffey Jr., not with plans for parades and victory celebrations.

One of the big reasons for the success was the

performance of Sasaki, who capped his big season by easily winning the AL Rookie of the Year award. The call came when he was back in Japan, touring the country as part of a major league All-Star team.

He received seventeen of the twenty-eight first-place votes to win the award over Oakland's Terrence Long. There was some debate about whether Sasaki, because of his ten years of professional experience in Japan, should be eligible for the award, but most of the voters didn't see that as an obstacle.

After all, Nomo had won the NL award when he was a rookie with the Dodgers in 1995. At thirty-two, Sasaki became the second oldest rookie to ever win the award. Sam Jethroe was also thirty-two when he was the NL Rookie of the Year for the Boston Braves in 1950 after several years in the Negro League, but he was thirty-three days older than Sasaki.

Sasaki's first year was not without a few missteps. In addition to his short pitching funk in May, Sasaki once turned the wrong way down a one-way street in Seattle (he turned around without incident) and occasionally misinterpreted his catcher's signs. In all, however, the year was a resounding success, personally and for the team.

"The first year is the toughest," said teammate Edgar Martinez, remembering his first year when he did not speak English. "After that you slowly become more comfortable. It can be tough when you don't have anyone else from your culture on the team, but he has an interpreter who's doing a good job with him. He's always in good spirits. That's a good sign."

Sasaki's spirits were lifted even higher when the Mariners landed another Japanese superstar, Ichiro Suzuki, before the 2001 season began. Not only did it mean that he would have a teammate from his native land, it meant someone else would be the focus of most of the Japanese media's stories in 2001.

The presence of both Japanese stars on the same team produced an onslaught of Japanese reporters at spring training. On the opening day of camp, ninety-seven reporters were present, eighty-five of whom were from Japan.

"It's like having two Michael Jordans on one team," Heid said. "They're not just big sports personalities. It goes beyond that. Some people would compare them to Elvis."

Big stars, no matter if they are in sports or entertainment, like to perform on the big stage. As Sasaki began spring training in 2001, he couldn't help but reflect on his rookie season, and he kept coming back to one moment.

He was sitting in the bullpen at Yankee Stadium during game 6 of the American League Championship Series. He was hoping his teammates would give him a chance to save the game and put the Mariners a win away from the World Series, but he had to sit and watch as the Yankees scored six runs in the seventh inning to turn a 4 to 3 Seattle lead into a 9 to 4 deficit. The Mariners did rally but still lost, 9 to 7, and Sasaki's season ended with him still in the bullpen.

"The awards were nice, I was happy to get them," Sasaki said. "But the real feeling I have from last year was losing out at the end of the season to the Yankees. It was a bittersweet season because of that. It left me feeling sad. It wasn't a good feeling."

Apparently, much of the Mariners' squad felt the same way. They began the 2001 season as if they were never going to lose a game. They posted a 20 to 5 record in April, the first major league team to ever win twenty games in April, and didn't lose back-to-back games until April 29 and May 1. They had the two longest winning streaks in club history, fifteen and nine games, early in the season, and their record of 38 and 12 was tied for the tenth best record after fifty games in baseball history. It was the best start since the 1984 Tigers went 39 and 11 in their first fifty games en route to the World Series championship.

Sasaki, of course, played a major role in that success. He set a major league record with thirteen saves in April, which also was a club record for saves in any month. He recorded saves in nineteen of his first twenty-four appearances of the year.

He spent much of his time in the spring trying

to develop a changeup and a two-seam fastball to augment his forkball and straight four-seam fast-ball.

"The hitters know what I throw now, so I have to stay a step ahead of them," he said in the spring. "I've worked very hard to add these pitches, so I will be able to throw the hitters something a little bit different.

"Everything will depend on the situation. I've learned from last year that I need to have those pitches. This spring I think I've shown that I have the confidence to throw these pitches."

The additional pitches may have given Sasaki more weapons at his disposal, but one thing about his game that didn't change in his second season was his enjoyment level and the way he displayed his emotions.

"Kaz wears his emotions on his sleeve, win or lose," Price said. "I like the fact that he doesn't have a façade. He doesn't try to be this intimidating guy. His stuff is intimidating enough. His success ratio is intimidating enough that he doesn't have to carve himself into a Fu Manchu and snarl at the hitters and blow spit and snot all over the place."

Sasaki told the *Seattle Times* early in the 2001 season, "All the things you have to do to prepare yourself for a save are very hard. Every save is very hard. There are times when I'm not feeling very good and I don't want to go out there, so of course it depends on the day. But any opportunity I can get, I will be out there.

"After I'm able to save the game, I'm so relieved and that's what people see. I'm just relieved and happy."

Like all closers, however, there are going to be nights when he hangs a pitch or even makes a good pitch and a good major league hitter does what he is supposed to do and delivers a home run or an RBI that costs Sasaki a save and the Mariners a win. The good closers, the ones who are the most successful, are the ones who can deal with those nights just as effectively as the nights when the outs come one, two, three.

"The one common thread among closers is you have to be able to be on the mound in the ninth inning of a game, with the game in your hands and be comfortable with that," Price told the *Seattle Times*. "You can't let the circumstance affect who you are as a pitcher.

"Good closers universally are very aggressive-minded people. I mean that in a good way, in a competitive way. That's what Kazu's all about. He's about me against you and I'm not backing down."

That is especially true on those occasions when Sasaki does not convert a save opportunity. He can't wait until the next game, wanting the ball again in exactly the same situation. He isn't likely to make the same mistake twice.

"I have a lot of respect for his integrity as a pitcher," Price said. "He's been a very impressive guy. He bends a little bit with a couple of base hits or a walk, but he very rarely breaks."

Another challenge that Sasaki was able to meet and pass this year was when he had to face his good friend and former teammate, Alex Rodriguez, with a game on the line. Rodriguez and Sasaki became close during the 2000 season, and it was tough for Sasaki to watch his friend leave as a free agent and sign with the Texas Rangers.

"We talked all the time," Sasaki said. "He made a lot of things clear to me. He helped me with everything there is about baseball. I'm sad that Alex is gone."

Still, he looked forward to the challenge of facing Rodriguez and getting him out.

They faced each other three times during the first eight games the Mariners played against Texas this season, and each time Sasaki came out on top.

"It was very difficult to pitch against him, because he's a friend," Sasaki said. "And the thing is, even if he wasn't a friend, he's a very difficult hitter to get out."

The knowledge of whom he is facing and how to get him out is coming easier to Sasaki now. A year and a half in the majors have convinced him of his ability, and his performance through the first part of this season put him on a pace to shatter the single-season save record of fifty-seven, set by

Bobby Thigpen of the White Sox in 1990. Through the Mariners' first sixty-four games, Sasaki had twenty-five saves, a pace that would give him sixty-three for the season. His chances of getting the record were increased by the fact that the Mariners were a winning team, they played a lot of close games, and he had good setup relievers who could get the ball to him with a lead in the ninth inning.

Sasaki's success, perhaps because it was expected after his rookie season, has not produced as many headlines and as much media attention as one might anticipate. This year those headlines and stories were going to another Japanese player, the Mariner's new right fielder, Ichiro Suzuki. Much as Sasaki came to the rescue to replace the departed Johnson and Griffey, it was Ichiro's arrival that had many Seattle fans asking: Alex who?

CHAPTER 5

Ichiro

Ichiro Suzuki faced a different challenge from all of the other Japanese players who had come before him. They had all been pitchers. No position player had ever made the transition from playing in Japan to playing in the major leagues.

One of the biggest concerns about position players making the switch was due to the difference in the two games. Whereas pitchers could still work approximately the same number of starts or pitch in relief an inning or so a game, position players face the extra burden of a longer season, more strenuous travel, and more pitchers to learn.

Most of the successful Japanese players also were not physically intimidating, more closely resembling Ichiro's stature. He is 5 foot 9 and weighs only 160 pounds.

One of the Japanese who questioned how well Ichiro would do in the major leagues was his future teammate, Kazuhiro Sasaki.

When Sasaki was back in Japan as part of the major league All-Star tour in November 2000, a reporter asked him about Ichiro's rumored move to the majors.

"Ichiro definitely has the technique, but he's also going to need some more strength physically, since the season is so long, and he will need some mental toughness as well," Sasaki said.

Ichiro knew the risks and thought he was ready for the challenge. He was not jumping to the majors blind. He actually had spent time in the Mariners' camp in spring training in 1999 as part of an exchange program between the Japanese and U.S. leagues.

While Ichiro was watching and learning from the Americans, they were watching and learning from, and about, him. Just as years ago baseball started recruiting and signing players from Latin America and other countries, it seemed only a matter of time before Japanese players were added to the mix.

The exposure of having Ichiro and other members of his Orix Blue Wave team in camp also helped spread the Mariners' popularity throughout Japan. Even though they were there for only two weeks, nearly a hundred Japanese media were on hand for the training camp, and the first spring game between the Mariners and Padres was televised live back to Japan.

"He's a good-looking athlete," said Mariners' manager Lou Piniella after getting his first look at Ichiro. "You can tell he's a pro by the way he goes about his business. He wasn't nervous. He was having fun.

"He does just about everything we try to get our

hitters to do. He keeps his hands back, and uses his legs and the lower half of his body. He is very compact in the hitting area. You can see why this kid has been successful."

The Mariners were also able to enjoy the visit by Ichiro and the other two Japanese players because they knew there was no way they would be able to sign them for at least two more years. Having played seven years in Japan, Ichiro was not scheduled to become a free agent until after the 2001 season.

Still, there were those in the Seattle organization who definitely made a note in their files to stay in touch. As one Seattle newspaper columnist noted after watching Ichiro for those few days, "They've [the Mariners] waited this long to fill left field and the leadoff spots, what's three more years?"

Playing those few spring games, as well as facing the Mariners' pitchers during batting practice drills, gave Ichiro a bit of an idea of what he was going to face from American pitchers when he was ready to make the jump to the major leagues.

As Jim Colborn noted, in Japan pitchers were more concerned about the location of their pitches than the movement of the pitches. That was an adjustment Ichiro knew he would have to make.

Ichiro did not get quite as much experience as he had hoped, because he was forced to sit out the final two games of his two-week stay, suffering from the stomach flu. As he boarded a flight home to Japan, however, he had no doubt he would be returning again some day in the not too distant future.

Indeed, when Sasaki signed with the Mariners in November 1999, he reportedly phoned Ichiro, saying he would lead the way to Seattle and "you can follow."

The Mariners learned late in the 2000 season that Ichiro was going to be allowed to go through the same posting system by which they were able to sign Sasaki the previous year. The owner of the Orix Blue Wave obviously realized Ichiro intended to leave when he was eligible for free agency.

If the owner was going to get anything for him, it would be wise to use the posting system and let teams bid for the right to sign Ichiro a year before he could leave on his own. The Mariners were of course very interested, but they knew they would not be alone.

The Mariners knew this was no ordinary player. Ichiro won his seventh consecutive batting title in Japan in 2000, hitting .387, which raised his career mark to .353. At age twenty-seven, he was just entering his prime.

The problems for the Mariners and the other clubs interested in Ichiro were threefold. First, they had to determine what his value was going to be. The way the posting rules work is that the team, in this case Orix, accepts all bids for their player, then decides which one it is willing to accept. If no team meets the undisclosed price Orix is seeking, Orix closes the bidding and Ichiro remains on its roster for another season.

The Mariners and other clubs also had to try to play the poker game with each other to find out what the other teams were going to be bidding. Since all bids were sealed, there was no way to top a bid by adding more money at the end.

Finally, even if the Mariners or another team made a bid that was accepted by Orix, it then had to negotiate and sign a contract with Ichiro. The teams had to determine how much money they thought that was going to take and see if they could work it into their budget. It was not a simple process.

At the same time, the Mariners were trying to negotiate and re-sign their own free agent, Alex Rodriguez, so they really didn't know for certain how much money they had to spend.

The figure they arrived at for their bid to Orix was $13.125 million. They thought it would be enough to satisfy the Orix owners, but they had to wait to find out if another major league club had outbid them. They knew there was interest from many clubs, including the Mets. Because of Valentine's experience in Japan, the Mets were well aware of Ichiro and his abilities.

Ichiro's popularity in Japan can be seen by the name he wore on the back of his jersey—Ichiro, his first name. In Japan he was as famous as Elvis and Tiger were in the United States.

On November 9 the Mariners received the phone call they had been waiting for. Orix had accepted their bid. They now had an exclusive thirty-day window to negotiate a contract with Ichiro and his agent, Tony Attanasio.

"The bid is merely an opportunity to get on the dance floor," said Mariners' chairman Howard Lincoln. "We have been very interested in Suzuki. We wanted to make sure we won the bidding. There was competition. We won."

Ichiro had dinner with Sasaki during the All-Star trip to Japan, even before he knew they would be future teammates. Sasaki told him there were three negatives to making the jump to the major leagues that he needed to be aware of.

"One is you have to get used to the food," Attanasio reported of that conversation. "Another is the travel is a lot more wearying on the body than he ever thought it would be. The third is that the caliber of play is different. Players are bigger, stronger, and they do things they don't do in Japan."

Attanasio admitted he had steered Sasaki to Seattle the previous year because he thought it was the right place for him to play. He had no influence on which team won the bidding for Ichiro's rights, but he was clearly pleased it turned out to be the Mariners.

"Clearly this is a club to which he wanted to go," Attanasio said. "This club, as demonstrated by their gesture and putting the money up front, wanted him. When those things happen, usually you're able to come to an agreement. This is an ideal situation for the club and player. It's the responsibility of both sides to get together somehow and some way. I would think something should be able to get done."

There was no official announcement on how many teams submitted formal bids for Ichiro's negotiating rights. Believed to be involved were the Mets, Tigers, Indians, Red Sox, and Dodgers. Reportedly the Dodgers submitted the second-highest bid of about $8 million.

The Mets were the team most disappointed that they didn't get Ichiro. Valentine has called Ichiro one of the five best players in the world.

"What I said, without a doubt, is that he'd be Rookie of the Year," Valentine said. "I thought he'd lead the league in triples. And I thought he'd hit in the high .300s. I also said that before the year was over, someone will say that he has the best arm, someone will say he is the best hitter, someone will say that he is the best defensive player, someone will say that he is the fastest runner."

Still, the Mets were more conservative in their bid for Ichiro than the Mariners.

"You couldn't see him play on a consistent basis and not say to yourself, 'There's something unbelievable about this guy. He's magic,' " Attanasio told *The Sporting News*. "Over there, he was hitting third and fourth. You could picture him as a leadoff guy, doing the things he's doing. Bobby [Valentine] knew that. Any international scout worth a nickel knew that. The problem was the blind bid."

Said Mets' chief executive officer Fred Wilpon, "They valued the player differently than anybody else in baseball. And they were right."

Winning the rights to negotiate with Ichiro didn't mean anything unless the Mariners were able to reach an agreement on a contract. It took less than ten days for that to happen, with Ichiro agreeing to a three-year deal worth between $15 million and $18 million.

Colborn said that despite good feelings on both sides about the contract being completed, there still were doubts about how successful Ichiro would be, primarily because of the pressure he would be under.

"He's trying to do something no Japanese has done before, not a position player," Colborn told the *Seattle Times*. "It's one thing for a pitcher to make the jump; a good arm is a good arm, and you sometimes see 20- and 21-year-old American kids make a successful move up to the majors because they have one.

"But it's much, much tougher for an everyday player. He has to handle the everyday challenge, hitting, hitting different styles of pitching, picking up signs, base running, defense.

"There is no telling how he really will adjust, but there is plenty of evidence he can and will. When he came back to Japan after being in camp with us in 1999, he felt he had not shown his best. So he really focused and in one nine-game period I watched him right after that, he had one swing-and-miss and two foul balls, and he hit every ball on the screws. They weren't all hits, but they were all hammered."

That was the kind of talk the Mariners and their fans wanted to hear, and when Ichiro made his first visit to Seattle and to Safeco Field, the media turned out as if the team were in the World Series.

Ichiro was taking his first look at the playing field at the same time a group of Japanese school-girls were getting a tour of the facility. When the girls saw Ichiro, they started screaming.

The Mariners thought they knew what they were getting in Ichiro, and at least initially in terms of reaction in Japan, they were right. Now they had to see what was going to happen on the field. All they could rely on was the experience of what he had done in the past.

Brian Raabe played against Ichiro in Japan in 1998, and he quickly noticed the respect opponents had for Ichiro.

"We intentionally walked him twice a game, regularly," Raabe said. "Any type of situation where he could hurt us, we walked him. We never let him swing a bat."

It took Ichiro years to achieve that kind of respect in Japan. "I started playing when I was three years old and I've played hard," Ichiro said through an interpreter.

Born in the Aichi Prefecture, Ichiro grew up in Toyoyama, on the island of Honshu, which is about 150 miles southwest of Tokyo. It is a suburb of Nagoya, the capital of Aichi Prefecture.

Ichiro was eight years old when he joined his first organized team, coached by his father. The games were only on Sunday, but Ichiro and his father could often be seen during the week working on developing his hitting, fielding, and pitching skills. That practice continued until Ichiro reached high school, where he became a standout pitcher. Clocked with a 93-mph fastball, Ichiro led his school, Aiko-Dai Meiden, to the prestigious Koushien tournament. Even though his team didn't win, Ichiro was able to impress numerous scouts who attended the games.

Some of the teams thought he had enough talent to become a pitcher, but at least one, the Orix Blue Wave, which plays in Kobe, liked his hitting ability better. He was selected by Orix in the fourth round of the 1991 Japan draft.

"I heard other teams wanted to draft him as a pitcher, but we were the only ones considering him as an outfielder," said Hide Sueyoshi, now the Mariners' assistant director of professional and international scouting who at the time was working for Orix. He also often serves as an interpreter for Ichiro.

Sueyoshi said it is not unusual for Japanese boys to put as much effort into baseball as Ichiro did. The one difference Sueyoshi has seen between the Little League equivalents in Japan and in the United States is that, in Japan, children are expected to specialize in one sport and devote all of their training to it, at a much earlier age than in the United States.

For most youngsters growing up when Ichiro did, the sport of choice was usually baseball, because of their fathers' interest in the game. Ichiro's father was no different. Working in a plant manufacturing small industrial mechanical parts by day, he turned his attention to baseball at night and on the weekends.

"In our father's generation, baseball was huge," Sueyoshi said. "They would work in the daytime, then watch games in the evening. They would laugh and cry for their team if they won or lost. It was always a father's dream for his boy to be a baseball player."

Those dreams came true in 1992, when Ichiro joined Orix. He spent much of his first two years playing for the Orix minor league team, where he hit .366 in fifty-eight games in 1992, then hit .371 with eight homers in forty-eight games in 1993 before he was called up to the major league team to stay.

Despite that success at the lower level, nobody was predicting that 1994 would be the year Ichiro would become a star. One who didn't think highly of Ichiro was Shozo Doi, who was the manager of the Orix major league team in 1992 and 1993. He didn't like Ichiro's batting style, which features a pendulum swing, and he didn't like Ichiro's tendency to shuffle his feet in the batter's box as the ball is coming toward the plate.

Doi reportedly said to Ichiro, "You'll never hit that way."

Doi was gone before the 1994 season, however, replaced as manager by Akira Ogi. Ogi did not share Doi's opinions about Ichiro's ability, believing instead that his style allowed him to make last-second adjustments as the pitch was coming toward the plate. He put Ichiro in the lineup and let the results speak for themselves.

Ichiro became the first Japanese player to surpass 200 hits in a season, finishing with 210 in the 130-game year. Almost forgotten was the fact that during that remarkable season he turned twenty. Ichiro finished with a then–Pacific League record .385 average. In addition to winning the batting title, he hit thirteen home runs, drove in fifty-four, and stole twenty-nine bases, being named the Pacific League's MVP.

He led the league with a .445 on-base average,

and in one stretch from May 21 to August 26, he reached base safely in sixty-nine consecutive games.

That was also the year he decided to drop his last name, Suzuki, and be known only by his first name, Ichiro. A common name in Japan, translated it means "number-one son."

Ichiro's popularity in Japan has grown ever since. In 1995 he was named Pacific League MVP for the second consecutive year and led Orix to the league championship and a spot in the Japan Series. His average dropped to .342, still good enough to lead the league, and he hit a career-high twenty-five homers and led the league with eighty RBIs and a career-high forty-nine stolen bases.

The following year he led Orix back to the Japan Series, and this time the Blue Wave won the championship. It was another MVP season for Ichiro, his third in a row, and another batting title, also number three, this time with a .356 average. In 1997, en route to his fourth consecutive batting title, Ichiro made a record 216 consecutive plate appearances, between April 16 and June 25, without striking out.

That span covered approximately fifty games, or roughly 40 percent of the season.

Another example of the kind of bat control Ichiro was showing at that point in his career came one day when he hit a single to center field off a pitch that bounced off the ground before he hit it.

It was about the time when he won another batting title in 1998, his fifth in succession, that Ichiro began to think more seriously about trying to make the jump to the major leagues when he had the chance. He was part of the opposition for a U.S. All-Star tour after the season, and he admitted to reporters that he was preparing for the move.

"I want to be the first player to show what Japanese batters can do in the United States," Ichiro said through an interpreter. "I'd like to go right away, but I'm not a free agent."

The *New York Daily News* reported that Ichiro was using the series against the U.S. stars as an attempt to showcase his skills.

"He nearly beat out a routine ground ball to second base in the first game of the series," the *Daily News* reported. "He twice stole second and third in the same inning in the first two games."

Ichiro said, "I don't need to be the number one player to be there. I'd just like to play at the highest level in the world. That's my dream at this point."

His spring training visit to the Mariners' camp in 1999 only increased Ichiro's desire, and he spent much of the 1999 season talking with American players in Japan about the differences between the two games and seeking advice on what he would have to do differently to be successful in the major leagues.

He asked about the tendencies of American pitchers. After he made a subtle change in his bat-

The Seattle Mariners' Ichiro Suzuki, at bat against the Milwaukee Brewers in a March, 2001 exhibition game. *AP/Wide World Photos*

Ichiro Suzuki rounds third to score in the seventh inning against the Oakland Athletics April 2, 2001, in Seattle. Suzuki, who singled earlier in the inning, scored on a single by teammate Edgar Martinez.
AP/Wide World Photos

Seattle Mariners relief pitcher Kazuhiro Sasaki reacts after the last out against the New York Yankees in Game 5 of the American League Championship Series, October 15, 2000. The Mariners defeated the Yankees 6-2. *AP/Wide World Photos*

Kazuhiro Sasaki in a March, 2000 exhibition game against the San Diego Padres. *AP/Wide World Photos*

Hideo Nomo, from his early days with the Los Angeles Dodgers. *Courtesy of the Los Angeles Dodgers*

Nomo celebrates after he pitches the Dodgers to a 7-2 victory over the San Diego Padres to clinch the 1995 Western Division title. Nomo was the 1995 N.L. Rookie of the Year. *Courtesy of the Los Angeles Dodgers*

Tsuyoshi Shinjo takes a cut. *David Seelig/Icon SMI*

The hard-hitting outfielder for the New York Mets.
David Seelig/Icon SMI

Masanori Murakami of the San Francisco Giants.
Courtesy of the San Francisco Giants

ting style, reducing the lift in his front foot, he found he was still able to drive the ball.

Ichiro hit a league-leading .343 in 1999, even though his season ended in late August when he suffered a broken bone in his right hand after being hit by a pitch. Knowing 2000 was going to be his final year in Japan, Ichiro was determined to go out on top. He actually was hitting .401 as late as July, before a late-season rib cage muscle pull ended his attempt to be the first Japanese hitter ever to top the .400 mark. He finished the year at a career-best .387. The only higher average in Japan history was .389, by American import Randy Bass in 1986.

During his seven consecutive batting titles, Ichiro hit. 385, .342, .356, .345, .358, .343, and .387. He reached 1,000 career hits faster than any hitter in Japanese history, and his career average was .353. Research found that the longest stretch he went in those seven years without getting a hit was fifteen at-bats. He won seven consecutive Gold Gloves and was named to the All-Star team seven years in a row.

With his increased success came added exposure and recognition. He became a superstar in Japan, known to everyone, not just baseball fans. When he came up to bat, camera flashbulbs went off all over the stadium, as they did in the United States during the home run chase by Mark McGwire and Sammy Sosa.

He is credited with renewing interest in baseball

among youngsters. The most recent high school tournament featured a record 4,150 high schools participating. His memorabilia and souvenirs were everywhere. His face was plastered on billboards all over Japan. He helped to improve the financial picture for Japanese players and to change the rules, giving them more freedom.

Ichiro attracted so much attention from the media, in fact, that when he and his fiancée, a television commentator in Japan, were planning their wedding, they decided to get married in Los Angeles so they would be able to have some privacy. The couple flew to Los Angeles separately, under assumed names, so only their few invited friends would know they were there.

One story about the media's infatuation with the couple noted that Ichiro once rolled himself up in a carpet stuffed in the back of a pickup truck so he could get past a crowd of reporters to go on a date with his future wife.

"It's fanaticism," Attanasio told the *Seattle Times*. "You can't have a dinner at a restaurant unless it's in a guarded private room. Otherwise, it would be impossible for him to eat.

"He can't walk into a [hotel] lobby. He would be mobbed. It's service entrances 100 percent of the time. His face and image are so identifiable. Take Mark McGwire's presence in this country, then multiply it by 100 or even 200 times, and you might get the idea what it's like for him there. I've been in this business a long time and have been around some of the biggest stars, but I've never seen a player in any sport treated that way."

Heid has been quoted as saying that "I've seen people grab their hearts when they see him. It's like they're having heart attacks. Japanese people will come to the United States to get close to him, because you can get closer to athletes in America. In Japan, they're much more guarded."

Even if the public can't get as close to athletes in Japan as they do in the United States, the public still is aware of what they are doing almost all of the time.

Colborn tells the story of Ichiro's news conference after the Mariners had reached an agreement on his contract. When he got into a taxi and asked the driver to take him to the Nintendo headquarters (for the news conference), the driver said, "Oh, you're going to the Ichiro press conference?"

Colborn asked the driver how he knew about the news conference. "He told me, 'Everybody knows. People may not know who the premier of the country is, but everyone from 3 to 93 knows Ichiro.' "

That was the kind of daily environment that existed for Ichiro in Japan and one of the reasons he looked forward to coming to the United States.

"In Japan, the media invaded my privacy so much," Ichiro told *ESPN Magazine*. "They would even watch me go to the haircut place or the restaurant. Then they would interview the people at the haircutters."

The reaction in Japan to Ichiro's imminent departure was mixed. While most fans were sorry to see him leave, they were excited to see how he would perform in the United States. Because of the coverage the Mariners' games would receive—almost all would be broadcast live on radio or television—most fans knew they would be able to follow Ichiro's progress with little difficulty.

There also was a feeling, as there had been with Sasaki, that he had done all he could in Japan, had fulfilled his contract, and was not disparaging the Japan League or his homeland by leaving. Ichiro said through an interpreter he didn't think his departure would have a negative impact on the Japan League. "I go, but another star soon will replace me," he said. "This is good for the younger generation."

When he worked out in early January before leaving for the United States, the media was there to watch him spend about an hour playing catch and hitting off a pitching machine.

"I have no idea what it is going to be like playing in the majors this year," Ichiro said. "I can only imagine what it might be like, so I will just have to go there and experience it."

Ichiro was ready for the Mariners, and they were ready for him.

———

Getting into the playoffs as the wildcard team in 2000 had been a great achievement for the Mariners and had helped them keep, and even acquire new, fans who were disappointed by the trades of free-agents-to-be Randy Johnson and Ken Griffey Jr.

The winter of 2000–2001 provided even more discontent for Mariners' fans, as free agent shortstop Alex Rodriguez, considered by many to be the best player in the game, left Seattle to sign a $252 million, ten-year contract with the Texas Rangers.

The club had survived the loss of Johnson and Griffey, getting some quality players in return, but how would they replace Rodriguez? When Ichiro signed, Rodriguez technically had not yet left the Mariners, but general manager Pat Gillick was prepared for him to leave.

"We got Ichiro before Alex left, but anticipating that Alex would go," Gillick said. "After Alex left, we signed [Bret] Boone. The two surprises offensively for us have been the leadoff hitter [Ichiro] and Booney. We were short last year offensively, and we were concerned we were going to be short again. But Ichiro and Boone have made up for a lot of it."

Gillick had seen Ichiro only on videotape prior to his first putting on a Mariners' uniform. Even that exposure was more than most fans in Seattle had seen of Ichiro, but they quickly took a liking to their newest player and wanted to do whatever they could to make him feel at home.

Especially in the Japanese community in Seattle, the arrival of Ichiro was greeted with great enthusiasm. The owner of a Japanese grocery store got a list of Ichiro's favorite Japanese delicacies and began to stock them. Such items as beef tongue, Pocari Sweat drink, BlackBlack chewing gum, and Boss coffee might not be on most Americans' shopping lists, but having those items available definitely made Ichiro feel more at home.

A restaurant in suburban Bellevue named one of its sushi offerings "Ichiro." He also was able to have some amount of privacy during his weeks in Seattle before reporting to spring training, something he was not accustomed to in Japan.

As the days dwindled toward the start of spring training, he was even more excited and eager to begin playing.

"I will never regret the fact that I came here to play baseball," he said through an interpreter. "I always had the dream to do this. Now I've done it. The only regret would be if I'd had the chance to come and hadn't."

Initially the Mariners' plans were to hit Ichiro third in their order, replacing Rodriguez. Even though Ichiro had always batted leadoff in Japan, Piniella thought the third spot was the best position for him in their lineup. Ichiro said he would do what the manager asked, but he was hoping to remain at the top of the batting order.

That would be decided during the exhibition games. The first order of spring training was conditioning, and the normal drills, which are about as interesting to the media as watching paint dry—the only people there are the ones who have to be.

On the first day that Ichiro wore a Mariners' uniform, ninety-seven reporters and photographers showed up. Eighty-five were from Japan.

"From the beginning of the day until the end, everyone is watching every move I make, taking pictures, asking for interviews," Ichiro said through his interpreter. "I understand everyone has a job to do. But don't you think they could just take a little break?"

One of the questions being asked over and over again was what Ichiro thought the biggest challenge of moving to the major leagues would be. Each time he gave essentially the same answer.

"I think the American strike zone will be the biggest adjustment," he said. "Everyone knows one thing for sure, and that's the American strike zone is bigger, wider than in Japan."

The other big day for Ichiro in spring training came when the Mariners actually played a game, losing the exhibition opener to the Padres. Ichiro played four innings, going one for three.

More than getting the first game out of the way,

he was happy to get the first-game postgame interviews over with.

The Mariners, because of their experience with Sasaki the previous year, knew what the media mob would be like. They were prepared for it, and Ichiro was prepared for it. He knows how popular he is in Japan and how every newspaper, magazine or television show wants to follow his every move in the United States. It is major news.

What the Mariners were more interested in seeing was what Ichiro could do on the field. They had their own expectations, but seeing him in person was the best way to gauge how good a player he was going to be.

"He's a very, very good defensive outfielder, above-average throwing arm, above-average runner," Gillick said. "Those tools we can count on. We know they're there. Now the situation is if he'll hit in the U.S. But he has hit for a number of years in Japan, and we're confident that will carry over in the U.S."

The Mariners adopted much of the same philosophy in letting Ichiro prepare for the season as they had done with Sasaki the previous year. Because he wasn't really a rookie and had years of experience to fall back on, they basically let him train and prepare the way he wanted to, working on what he felt was important. The numbers didn't matter to them, and they were willing to let Ichiro dictate how he wanted to handle the daily media on-slaught.

One month into camp, he admitted the media attention had been greater than even he had expected.

"Baseball has been the greatest thing in my life, but the cameras and the media surrounding baseball have not been fun," he said. "I kind of expected the sheer numbers. I didn't expect them to watch every move I make, from the time I get to the parking lot to the time I leave the parking lot. It's unnecessary.

"How many times do they have to see me stretch? How many times do they have to see me walk?"

It was his running ability, not walking, that was the biggest surprise to Piniella and the Mariners during the spring. Ichiro was timed in under four seconds running to first and beat out grounders for infield hits that appeared to be routine outs. That was something scouts would put in their advance reports, forcing team defenses to make adjustments.

"Infielders are playing him shallower, so it's going to make it easier to get the ball through the infield," Piniella said.

That was one of the reasons why Piniella changed his mind about seeing if Ichiro could bat third and decided to leave him at the top of the order, hoping his speed would let him reach base and distract the defense and the pitcher.

The Mariners were not counting on much power from Ichiro, but Piniella was reassured when he saw the player pull a ball into right field for a home run on March 20. "Once you've seen it, you don't have to see it often to know he can do it," Piniella said.

That was basically the same reaction the Japanese media had with Ichiro's move to the majors. They had seen what he could do in Japan, and there was no reason to think he couldn't do the same thing in the United States. The pressure facing Ichiro, however, was to prove it.

"Everyone believes Ichiro can succeed in the major leagues," Yoichi Amari of the Sports Nippon Newspapers told the *Seattle Times*. "But if he doesn't succeed, then Japanese players will not play [here] again. He is the best player in Japan, so if he can't play, no one can."

Ichiro himself had no doubts. But he also was quick to point out that he was playing for the Mariners, not the country of Japan.

"Obviously, I am the first position player to come over, that's a given," Ichiro said through his interpreter. "People say I'm an explorer, a pioneer, whatever. That's other people's opinion. That's not why I came over here. I came over here to play baseball.

"I don't play baseball for other people. I play baseball for myself. They [reporters] can have whatever pressure they want to put on, but I don't feel it. I really don't have an idea what they are expecting me to do. I just play the best I can."

That was all the Mariners were asking, and it was clear they were expecting that to be pretty good. Three of the team's seven preseason television commercials featured Ichiro and Sasaki. Four games were scheduled for the regular season involving Ichiro or Sasaki giveaway promotions, including two bobblehead doll promotions.

The top-selling item by far in the Mariners' team stores was the replica Ichiro jersey. And he still had yet to play a regular season game.

The Mariners were waiting for that moment, and so, it turned out, was Ichiro. The Mariners admitted they were a little disappointed by what they saw from Ichiro during the spring. They had some doubts about whether he was as good as they had expected.

"I really thought after watching him all spring that he would be lucky to hit .300," Piniella told *Baseball Weekly*. "I would have settled for .280."

Once opening day arrived, however, it was an entirely different story.

The Mariners' opening day game against Oakland was telecast live in Japan—by two different networks. It also was broadcast live on radio. The crowd that turned out was the largest ever for a regular-season game at Safeco Field. Ichiro didn't disappoint any Mariners fans or his fans watching or listening in his native country.

He started a game-tying two-run rally in the seventh, then extended the winning rally in the eighth with his first bunt single in eight years. Seattle won 5 to 4, with Sasaki closing out the victory in the ninth inning.

"A few years ago, Kazuhiro talked about how great it would be to play on the same team, to have a good game and then have Kazu come in and save it," Ichiro said through his interpreter after the game. "To have all that in our very first game is unbelievable."

Ichiro had gone hitless in his first three at-bats before singling to center off reliever T. J. Mathews in the seventh. He later scored on a hit by Edgar Martinez as the Mariners rallied from a 4 to 2 deficit.

His drag bunt single in the eighth followed a walk to Carlos Guillen, who went to third when Oakland pitcher Jim Mecir and first baseman Jason Giambi mishandled the ball. Guillen then scored the winning run on a sacrifice fly by John Olerud, securing the first of what would turn out to be many Mariners' victories during the season.

One of the biggest reasons the night was so special for Ichiro was that his father, Nobuyuki Suzuki, was there, watching from a seat in the first row behind the Mariners' dugout.

Ichiro has always credited the work with his father while he was growing up as being one of the reasons he was able to succeed in both the Japan League and in the United States.

"He would take Ichiro to a nearby elementary school where they would use the field for playing catch and hitting, taking ground balls and running," Heid said. Afterward, Ichiro would go home and complete his homework, then the elder Suzuki would take his son to the batting cages.

In a statement issued by the Mariners, the elder Suzuki was quoted as saying "I wish Ichiro the best after his signing and that he keeps well in this situation of playing baseball in a very different world. I wish him well playing because it is his most favorite thing."

Nobody could have written a better script, not only for opening day but for the first several days of Ichiro's major league career. On Friday, April 6, Ichiro and the Mariners got their first look at Alex Rodriguez wearing an enemy uniform. All Ichiro did was open the game with a double, leading to a four-run first, then finish the game in the tenth with his first major league homer, his fourth hit of the night.

"For anyone watching the game, it was hard to see the 10 innings as anything other than Ichiro Time," reported the *Seattle Post-Intelligencer*. In his first four games, Ichiro was 8 for 19 (a .421 average) with a double, homer, five runs scored, and two RBIs.

Added to the list of believers was Texas manager Johnny Oates.

"All the tapes I saw of him showed that Suzuki plays the game the way it's supposed to be played," Oates said. "During each at-bat, he knew what to do at the plate. If they needed a man on base, he got on base. If they needed a fly ball, he hits the fly ball. Suzuki did everything he was supposed to do on the field."

Another interested observer to Ichiro's first week in the majors was Matsanori Murakami, the first Japanese player in the United States thirty-seven years ago. Murakami helped broadcast Ichiro's first three games back to Japan.

"Oh, he's good," Murakami said. "But it will take time."

The next scene in the quickly developing snapshots on the Ichiro highlight video came on April 11 in Oakland, when Ichiro got a chance to show off his throwing ability. Trying to advance from first to third on a single by Ramon Hernandez, Terrence Long was cut down by Ichiro's perfect throw. The out ended any thoughts of an Oakland comeback, securing Seattle's 3 to 0 win.

The play quickly earned a nickname—the Throw.

"I was going over to back up third base, so I didn't see the ball," said pitcher Aaron Sele. "By the time I got to my position, all of a sudden, the ball was in David's [Bell] glove."

The beat writers for the Seattle newspapers had to pull out their thesauruses looking for the right words to describe what they had just witnessed.

Wrote Bob Finnigan in the *Seattle Times*, "Think of the best throw you've ever seen and forget it. This had to be as good if not better, a 200-foot lightning bolt that was never more than a few feet off the ground."

John Hickey wrote in the *Seattle Post-Intelligencer*, "Ichiro came up with a throw from right field that needs to be framed and hung on the wall at the Louvre next to the Mona Lisa. It was that much a thing of beauty."

The play came one night after rowdy Oakland fans greeted Ichiro by throwing ice and coins at him from the stands. He didn't seem too perturbed, noting that he once had an aluminum can thrown at him during a road game in Japan.

Jay Buhner warned him that could happen in other cities as well; he also had been pelted with batteries, golf balls, and money during his career.

"The worst was New York," he said. "One night Junior [Griffey] and I collected $6.18 between us. I mean, you get 10 quarters, that's $2.50 right there."

Ichiro even prevailed in the first all-Japan match-up in the majors, collecting an infield single off the Angels' Shigetoshi Hasegawa, his former teammate in Orix, on April 13.

Piniella tried to offer a voice of reason to the

growing hype about Ichiro, but even he didn't sound too convincing.

"He's played 15 games," Piniella said on April 18. "He's gotten off to a good start. We're very pleased with him. But there's a lot of hurdles out there yet. To put super-human expectations on him would be self-defeating in purpose.

"Just let the guy relax. Let him get his at-bats. Keep on acclimating himself to the league. If we put the type of expectations on him here that he has on him in Japan, it would be very, very counterproductive."

By the time he had played fifteen games in the majors, Ichiro had already broken the team record for longest hitting streak by a rookie, which had been twelve games, set by Mickey Brantley in 1987. Less than three weeks into his career, Ichiro was already being called the best leadoff hitter in the history of the Mariners' franchise.

He also had to deal with another off-the-field distraction. Reports surfaced in mid-April that a Japanese publication was offering $2 million for a nude picture of Ichiro.

Nobody knew whether the report was true or false, but Ichiro's teammates made certain they had fun with the possibilities.

"I've already told him, 'Let me take the picture and we can share the money,' " Al Martin said.

Teams could joke about issues like that when they were off to the kind of start the Mariners were.

Seattle won eighteen of its first twenty-two games, quickly opening a huge lead in the AL West race.

Ichiro was seeing all of the stadiums he had heard about and seen only in pictures and on television, facing the pitchers he had wondered for years if he could hit. He played in Yankee Stadium. He couldn't wait for the Mariners' first visit to Fenway Park. He got the chance to face Roger Clemens and Pedro Martinez. All the time, he kept getting hits, making great throws, or taking home runs away from the opposition with a great catch.

The Mariners finished April with a 20 and 5 record, becoming the first major league club in history to win twenty games in April. Ichiro was named the American League's Rookie of the Month.

"He's the engine of our train right now," said center fielder Mike Cameron, and there was no indication that train was going to run out of steam any time soon.

Not mentioning Ichiro by name, Piniella agreed that he had been the catalyst for the team's amazing start. "It starts with our leadoff guy," he told *The Sporting News*. "He gets on base. He gets his hits. He scores runs for us. Those are the sorts of things that are contagious."

What was impressing not only those on his own team but opponents as well was how few times Ichiro swung and missed a pitch. In six games between the Blue Jays and Seattle, Toronto counted four times that Ichiro swung at and missed a pitch.

"The ability to make contact is just how I learned to hit," Ichiro said. "That's been a focus ever since I was a little player. That was important, and so I worked on it."

By the middle of May, Stats Inc. reported that Ichiro had swung and missed only twenty-two times in 275 swings.

"And [Ichiro] has faced a lot of tough pitchers who put the ball in hard places to hit," said first baseman John Olerud. "He doesn't know their tendencies or what they're trying to do to him, and yet he's still putting the ball in play. That's the amazing thing about him."

One strategy some pitchers tried to adopt in working to Ichiro was to jam him with inside fastballs, hoping he wouldn't be able to get his hands turned quickly enough to make solid contact on the ball. Toronto tried it, and he collected nine hits in three games.

"He's just such a pesky hitter," said his teammate, pitcher Jamie Moyer. "I've watched what teams have tried to do with him, and I don't know if there's a way to pitch to him. He hasn't shown yet that he has a glaring weakness. Regardless of what teams have done, he's hit them."

Ichiro also hit them in different ways, proving that he was not just a slap-the-ball-and-run kind of hitter. He always seems to know the game situation and what is called for, and that's the type of hit he tries to deliver.

"You'd never see an American kid try the things he does," Mariners' second baseman Bret Boone, the third generation of a major league family, told *ESPN Magazine*. "Some coach would put a stop to it in Little League. Most of us try to groove one swing. I think he's got about five different grooves, and he breaks out a different one depending on what the situation in the game is."

Not only was Ichiro on a pace to break the major league hit record of 257 set by George Sisler of the St. Louis Browns in 1920, he almost certainly was putting himself in a position to become only the third rookie in the last thirty-seven years to collect 200 or more hits in a season, joining Boston's Nomar Garciaparra in 1997 and Kevin Seitzer of the Royals in 1987. Rodriguez's team record of 215 hits set in 1996 also was in definite jeopardy, as was the major league rookie record of 223 hits set by Lloyd Waner of the Pirates in 1927.

The other hit record Ichiro seemed destined to challenge was the mark of getting a hit in the most games during the season, currently 135 games, accomplished three times, most recently by Wade Boggs in 1985.

Ichiro even got one of the Mariners' three hits in a 2 to 0 loss to Pedro Martinez and the Red Sox on May 1. In the game the following night that had all of Japan paying attention, he was 0 for 2 against Hideo Nomo before being plunked in the back by a pitch.

The name that kept coming up when people tried to find an American to compare Ichiro to was Ralph Garr, the former Braves and White Sox out-fielder who hit .306 over a thirteen year career.

"Ralph was a phenomenal player," said Toronto manager Buck Martinez. "He was a challenge for a pitcher all the time. He had good speed, could hit it all over the park and once in a while hit it out."

Piniella also agreed with the Garr comparison. "Gator [Garr's nickname] was a contact hitter," he said. "He used the whole field. He ran a little out of the box. He didn't strike out much. He didn't walk much. He hit an occasional home run but he had good gap power."

Garr himself saw the comparison. Now living in Houston, where he is a scout for the Braves, Garr told Larry Stone of the *Seattle Times* that his hitting style and that of Ichiro were similar.

"He bats completely offbeat, but he keeps his head in the hitting zone, regardless of what his body is doing," Garr said. "I was a lot similar. I was watching him on TV, stepping toward third and hitting the other way. That's what I did. It's a great comparison."

Seattle GM Pat Gillick, and others, brought up Boggs's name. Other suggestions included Rod Ca-rew and even Paul Waner, whose name was brought up by Hall of Famer Bobby Doerr, now eighty-three, who lives in Oregon and watches many of the Mariners' games on television.

By the time the Yankees came to Seattle for a three-game series on May 18, Ichiro had a twenty-two-game hitting streak. He also had at least one hit in thirty-eight of the Mariners' first forty games. With his hitting streaks of fifteen and twenty-two games, Ichiro joined Kent Hrbek of the Twins (1982) and Juan Pierre of the Rockies (2000) as the only major leaguers to have at least two fifteen-game or more hitting streaks in their rookie seasons.

In those first forty games, Ichiro hit .371. In comparisons researched by ESPN's Jayson Stark, of the five active hitters who began this year with a career average of .320 or higher and 3,000 or more career at-bats, only Frank Thomas of the White Sox was over .300 in the first forty games of his career. Of that group, Thomas again hit in the highest number of his first forty games, getting at least one hit twenty-nine times.

Tony Gwynn and Mike Piazza got a hit in twenty-eight of their first forty games. Derek Jeter got a hit in twenty-five of his first forty games, and Edgar Martinez in twenty-two of his first forty.

"It looks like he hits the ball exactly where he wants to," said Seattle hitting coach Gerald Perry.

Sports Illustrated's research found that the three hitters generally considered the best of this generation—Boggs, George Brett, and Gwynn—had streaks in which they had hits in thirty-nine out of forty-one games a combined four times in their collective fifty-nine seasons.

Ichiro was quickly gaining respect from his peers, players like Jeter who could not help but be impressed by the way Ichiro approached the game and his ability to succeed. Jeter said Ichiro was forcing defenses to play differently against him than other players.

"You can't think," Jeter said. "If you think on one of his ground balls then he's safe. Basically you have to charge it and try to get rid of it as soon as possible because he's the fastest guy in the league.

"I don't think there's really anyone to compare him to. He puts the ball in play, and if you go one step or two steps either way, then you might as well hold the ball because you're not going to throw him out."

Said Mariners' first-base coach John Moses, "I can't tell you how many first basemen I've heard yell 'hurry up, hurry up' to the infielders after Ichiro has hit a ground ball. They worry about him in every way. The infielders' eyes get about this big when he's up. If the shortstop is playing at normal depth, he almost has no chance."

In the first game against the Yankees, a three-hit night helped Ichiro extend his streak to twenty-three games, equaling the longest streak of his career in Japan. During his marvelous 1994 season with Orix, he had two twenty-three-game streaks. It was also his seventh consecutive multiple-hit game, tying a club record.

He singled in the second, then stole second and third. He had an RBI single in the fifth, then ran down a long fly ball in the seventh. When he bent down at second after doubling in the eight, Jeter walked by.

"Take it easy, man," Jeter told him. "That's enough."

After going 0 for 3 in his first three at-bats the following day, Ichiro came to bat in the eighth inning against Orlando Hernandez, possibly with the last chance to extend his streak. The Mariners led 1 to 0, and Kazuhiro Sasaki was warming up in the bullpen.

Hernandez hit Ichiro in the back with a fastball. The crowd booed as he trotted toward first. As it turned out, Sasaki gave up a run and the game went to the tenth, giving Ichiro an extra chance to extend the streak. This time, against Mariano Rivera, he grounded out to shortstop, keeping him one hit away from tying Joey Cora's team record twenty-four-game streak.

Ichiro wasn't concerned. "Someday it's going to be over and today's the day it's over," Ichiro said. "This is not the end of my career."

Indeed, Ichiro was confident he would start another streak the following day. He knows he is still learning, especially when he faces a pitcher for the first time. He does use video to scout upcoming pitchers and reads the scouting reports, but nothing prepares him more than actual at-bats.

"When I get up, I feel and get a sense of the pitcher," he told the *Seattle Times*. "I analyze what he might throw me, then I trust my sense of the pitcher and make the adjustment. I want to have the same pace and pattern here [as in Japan]. The more information I get on opposing pitchers the better my performance may be. I can observe and use that."

Each passing Mariners' game was becoming more of an event than a ballgame, something that was true in Seattle when Johnson pitched and how fans felt when watching Griffey and Rodriguez play.

"It's fun watching him play," Piniella said, "like it was with Junior and Alex and when Randy pitched. It's different, but just as productive in its own way."

One of the biggest differences, even though it was still the first half of the season, was that none of the teams featuring Johnson, Griffey, or Rodriguez was as successful as this Mariners' team. Before the season was two months old, Seattle had built a double-digit lead in the AL West.

As the baseball world began to focus more on the Mariners in general and Ichiro in particular, in came financial offers, all of which Ichiro turned down.

"In his mind, he hasn't done anything yet," said his agent, Attanasio. "He hasn't proven to himself that he can play in the major leagues on an every-day basis and accomplish what he wants to do.

"He doesn't want to say to the world 'Look how great I am.' He doesn't believe that yet. He's happy with what he has done, but he's not thrilled with it."

Ichiro might have been the only person expressing that sentiment. With each game and each passing series came more praise and raves from opponents and teammates about his hitting ability, a great throw, a great defensive play, or his speed on the bases.

"People talk about changing leagues, from National to American, being a challenge," said Minnesota coach and future Hall of Famer Paul Molitor. "This guy is seeing American baseball for the first time and hitting .360. That's pretty impressive."

Also impressive was the list of past and current baseball greats who came out specifically to meet, and collect an autograph from, Ichiro. There was Kirby Puckett in Minnesota. George Brett visited the Seattle clubhouse in Kansas City, bringing his two kids. Before he faced him later in the day, David Wells of the White Sox asked Ichiro for an autographed bat.

"I was surprised he wanted to meet me," Puckett told *Baseball Weekly*. "It's an honor, especially when it's a player who is making the kind of impact Ichiro is."

On the field before a game in Anaheim, Ichiro saw and recognized Mr. Cub, Ernie Banks, and made a special point of saying hello. In Kansas City, Ichiro didn't recognize Buck O'Neil, the former Negro League star, but he could tell that O'Neil was important and sought out information about him, then was very humbled to meet him.

His appreciation of the game's history and his respect for all of those who have come before him are reasons why Ichiro has quickly earned such favorable reviews from his fellow players.

That, and what he accomplished on the field in his first two months in the major leagues.

"I've never seen anyone like him," said the Yankees' Tino Martinez. "I don't even know where to play the guy—shallow, deep, somewhere in between—because I get the feeling he makes up his mind where to hit the ball and then puts it there. It's unreal."

American players also were amazed to watch just how closely Ichiro and the other Japanese stars are covered by members of the Japanese media. Those who don't like the American press would either wilt or snap if they had to exist with the same conditions of trying to please all of the Japanese media facing Ichiro and the rest of his countrymen.

In spring training, one Japanese reporter actually counted the number of swings Ichiro took in batting practice, then asked a Seattle coach if there was a problem because Ichiro had taken fewer swings than he had the previous day.

"I remember one game when Ichiro was on first and he took off on a 3-and-1 count and Mike Cameron swung and missed and Ichiro got thrown out," said Mark McLemore. "They asked Mike why he swung and missed and got Ichiro thrown out."

One Japanese cameraman was discussing the coverage of Ichiro before a game in Oakland, when he excused himself from the conversation so he could begin filming Ichiro—taking batting practice.

"He's got to deal with the Japanese media and the whole country watching him," McLemore said. "And he's got this country watching him. There's a lot of other things that go along with it that he's still able to do while in that fish bowl, or actually that petri dish. It's just totally amazing."

Of course, the whole story of Ichiro's success would be different if it was not running side by side with the success of the Mariners. The team followed its record-setting April by winning twenty games again in May, leaving it with a 40 and 12 record. On May 23 the team launched a fifteen-game winning streak, not losing the thirteenth game of the year until June 8.

Other players, including Bret Boone, John Olerud, Edgar Martinez, the starting pitchers, and the bullpen, were carrying their share of the load, but

more than one observer credited Ichiro with setting
the tone for the team.

"He's a phenomenal player," said Oakland's Jason Giambi, the reigning American League MVP.
"He makes that machine go. He puts pressure on
the defense, puts the ball in play and runs like hell.
Olerud, Edgar, and Boone—the seasons they're
having are because of him. He's the missing link."

What was driving Ichiro so hard is that he
doesn't believe he has reached his peak. He left
Japan because he wanted to see how he could perform against the best players in the world, in the
major leagues, and that is still an unanswered question in his mind.

That is why he continues to work so hard everyday, pushing himself and his team.

"I'm not satisfied with the way I'm hitting,"
Ichiro told the *Tacoma News-Tribune*. "I've never
been satisfied with it. To be satisfied is to stop
searching.

"They say you are successful in baseball if you
only fail 70 percent of the time, that going 3-for-
10 is successful. As long as I play, I will look for
a way to improve on that. If a pitcher beats me
seven out of 10 times, I can accept that. But if I
get myself out in some of those at-bats, that I can
improve on.

"What if I cut down on one, two outs in those
10 at-bats by doing something better? Cut your

mistakes, you improve. In this game, there's some-thing every day you can be disappointed with."

That striving for perfection is why Ichiro almost certainly will follow Sasaki as the American League Rookie of the Year. It could see him become only the second player in history to win the Rookie of the Year and the MVP award in the same season. Fred Lynn did that for Boston in 1975.

Lynn has been watching Ichiro on television from his home near San Diego.

"He's been sensational," Lynn told the *Seattle Times*. "When a guy comes in with the credentials he has, you know he's going to hit. The question is whether he can keep up the average he has, but it doesn't look like he's going to slow down any time soon."

That is why there was increasing speculation by many longtime baseball observers that not only could Ichiro be the Rookie of the Year and the MVP, he could be the player with the best chance of hitting .400 since Ted Williams in 1941 and the player with the best chance of challenging Joe DiMaggio's record fifty-six-game hitting streak.

According to Sueyoshi, Ichiro always hit better in Japan during the warm summer months, and he expects that to be the case with the Mariners as well. "The better the weather, the better he is," Sueyoshi said.

It was perhaps fitting that on the first day of summer, June 21, Ichiro got three hits in the Mariners' 12 to 10 win over Oakland, allowing him to raise his average to .356 and overtake Boston's Manny Ramirez for first place in the AL batting race.

When Piniella had been a guest earlier in the year on Rob Dibble's show on ESPN Radio, Dibble had said he would run naked through Times Square if Ichiro won the batting title.

"He better start working on his tan," Piniella said.

With All-Star game voting expanded to include Japan this year, it was no surprise that Ichiro was voted into the starting lineup. Nevertheless, few, if any, would have predicted that he would be the AL squad's leading vote getter. That was just another indication of how much he has accomplished in such a short time in the United States.

He has done it, too, without losing the respect and recognition that he had established in Japan. If anything, his success with the Mariners has gained him an even greater level of respect and appreciation from the baseball fans in his homeland.

What those fans most worry about, however, is what the success of Ichiro's and the other Japanese players will do to their professional game. Will more Japanese players try to leave their home teams and play in the major leagues? The opinion is mixed. Some fans say the biggest impact might be to change the style of play in Japan, making the Japanese game more like the game in the United States, faster, more dramatic.

There are, no doubt, other players in Japan with the skills necessary and the mental toughness who will try to make the jump to the major leagues. How close they come to matching Ichiro's level of success, only time will tell.

To most observers from Japan, the true measure of success for a Japanese player in the major leagues has nothing to do with Ichiro, however. He was a superstar in Japan, and they fully expected him to be a superstar in the United States. They look instead to Tsuyoshi Shinjo, who followed Ichiro's signing by leaving Japan to play for the New York Mets. Shinjo's career average for ten years in Japan was .249. How well would he do in the major leagues?

Ichiro proved to be a hit in his first All-Star game. He was the focus of much of the pre-game activity, having to disguise his identity and use secretive routes in and out of Safeco Field and the headquarters hotel, where his news conference produced arguments and fights among the media trying to get a better view of the celebrity.

At the break, he was tied for second in the AL batting race with a .347 average. His 134 hits was 16 more than any other hitter in the league, and he led in runs scored and was tied for the league lead in stolen bases.

The All-Star game was just another night for him to display all of his skills, and he did it in the very first inning. Batting against Randy Johnson,

Ichiro hit the second pitch down the first-base line. It appeared headed for the right-field corner, but Todd Helton made a diving stop. Still, Ichiro's speed allowed him to beat Johnson to first for a base hit. He then stole second base.

Ichiro was hitless in his next two at-bats before leaving the game, but the other Japanese player in the game, Sasaki, earned his place on the stage by pitching a perfect ninth inning to save the game for the American League.

CHAPTER 6

More Stars

Most observers considered the success or failure of Tsuyoshi Shinjo with the New York Mets as the true litmus test for the future of Japanese players in the major leagues.

Unlike Ichiro, who had won seven consecutive batting titles and was universally recognized as an outstanding player, Shinjo had not received anywhere near as much attention when he signed with the Mets in December 2000.

The opinion in Japan was that he was a good player but not great. He was considered an above-average outfielder, having won seven Gold Glove awards, but he had never hit higher than .278 in his ten years with the Hanshin Tigers. At twenty-nine, he was two years older than Ichiro.

Shinjo was coming off the best season of his Japanese League career, having earned his fourth All-Star selection and hitting a career-high twenty-eight homers with 85 RBI to go along with his .278 average in 131 games. He also stole a career-best fifteen bases.

Shinjo was the most popular player on the Tigers, and he turned down a reported five-year offer worth $12 million to sign a contract with the Mets worth a guaranteed $700,000, plus two option years. He also had discussions about joining other teams in Japan. Much like Ichiro, his goal in coming to the United States was to test his own abilities and find out if he was good enough to compete against the world's best players.

"I considered a number of things, but I think I've finally found a place where I can play the kind of baseball I'm capable of," Shinjo said when he announced he was signing with the Mets. "The feeling that I've wanted to play at such a high level as the major leagues has grown stronger in me the last five years. I don't know if I'll be successful or not, but I will do my best to follow my dream."

If Shinjo did prove capable of handling the jump, many believed that it could open the door for more Japanese players—and not just the superstars—to leave Japan and move to the major leagues.

The difference, of course, is that Shinjo had played long enough to qualify for free agency and did not have to go through the posting system, so there was no extra money that had to be paid to the club, and the club didn't have to give its blessing to Shinjo leaving.

Shinjo was one of the players Mets' manager Bobby Valentine had been watching since he'd managed in Japan in 1995. He thought the investment was a good one, even though he went to spring training not knowing exactly what role Shinjo would play on the Mets in the 2001 season.

"I've contended, and I could be proven wrong, that if players had the desire to play here, a Japanese hitter could succeed at the major league level," Valentine said.

Shinjo knew there were those who doubted he could be successful.

"Ten out of ten people have been telling me that I may not be able to make it here," he said through an interpreter on a December trip to New York. "I welcome those thoughts. What I have to do is prove myself during the season. If they're going to talk and continue to doubt my abilities, let them talk."

In 511 at-bats with Hanshin in 2000, Shinjo walked just thirty-two times and struck out ninety-three times. Scouts noted he was weak against breaking ball pitches, a red flag that did concern Mets' officials. Watching videotapes of Shinjo over the winter, they noted a particular stretch in which Shinjo saw eighty-five consecutive off-speed pitches.

When he reported to Port St. Lucie, Florida, for spring training, Shinjo was ready to show the Mets he could hit a fastball and that he could hit breaking balls better than they expected as well. He also was ready to show them that he knew nothing was going to be handed to him and that he was willing to work—a trait common to the Japanese—to make it a smooth transition.

After the morning workout on the first day of spring training, Shinjo reportedly asked Valentine what time he should return for the evening practice, not realizing the U.S. teams practiced only once a day during the spring. When told there was no other practice, Shinjo worked out alone, swinging a bat in the parking lot of the team's hotel.

In the middle of March, he was still being labeled as a "borderline outfield prospect" by the *New York Daily News*, which reported there was a chance he would not make the Mets' opening day roster. The fact that between thirty and forty Japanese reporters were present at the team's camp almost everyday, with the sole purpose of covering Shinjo, made his day-to-day progress much more of a story than if he been just another American trying to make the team.

"He's a good athlete, an excellent athlete," said Omar Minaya, the Mets' international scouting director. "He might have to go to the minors, but that would only be part of the process of becoming a major-leaguer. He understands that."

During the first week of camp, he was consistently popping balls up to all fields. But as the games began, he began to refine his swing and started producing base hits. By the last week of spring, as the final roster decisions were being made for opening day, Shinjo was hitting .375 with eight RBI as he locked up one of the spots for reserve outfielders on the team.

About his only disappointment in the spring was when he found out he would not be allowed to wear his signature red sweatbands on his wrists. Major league rules prohibit players from wearing nonteam colors, so Shinjo could choose from blue, black, orange, white, or gray sweat bands.

"I think all of the Japanese fans are going to be sad," Shinjo said.

"It might not mean much to fans in the United States, but asking Shinjo to abandon red is like asking Elvis to shave off his sideburns or asking Johnny Cash to wear yellow," the *New York Daily News* reported.

"I get letters from the fans saying they want to see Shinjo in red," the player said. "But I want to be part of the team, not stand out."

Stand out was what Shinjo did in Japan, even if he wasn't recognized as one of the country's superstar players. His picture was everywhere, he has done his share of modeling, and he was married to one of Japan's most popular models.

He has his own personal website and said he could not walk the streets in Japan without worrying about some member of the press taking his picture. Born in Fukuoka, Shinjo graduated from Nishinihon-Tandai Fuzoku High School and was selected by Hanshin in the fifth round of the 1989 draft. He broke into the Japan League in 1991, appearing in thirteen games, then began to play regularly in 1992.

He made the All-Star team for the first time in 1994 and proved to be a consistent, if not over-whelming, offensive player for seven seasons. His popularity off the field contributed greatly to his financial success, and that success was one of the reasons Valentine found it hard to believe Shinjo would want to leave Japan.

"You're playing at home," Valentine said. "You're being well paid. Everybody loves you. Why the hell would you want to come here?"

Shinjo showed why in the Mets' home opener against the Braves, when he hit a fastball into the back of the left center field bleachers for his first U.S. home run in a 9 to 4 New York win. Taking advantage of injuries to Benny Agbayani and Timo Perez, Shinjo moved into the starting lineup and began to deliver clutch hits.

He played through a sore muscle for more than a month, later telling friends that he thought he would lose "his place" if he told Valentine or other Mets' officials that he was hurt. The injury did fi-nally put him on the disabled list, but not before he had won over the Mets' fans with his flashy style and his penchant for getting big hits late in close games. In fact, Shinjo proved to be one of the few bright spots for the Mets in the first half of the season.

His RBI single with two outs in the bottom of the ninth gave the Mets a 6 to 5 win over the Dodg-ers on May 20. The following night it was a three-run double in the sixth against Montreal. Two nights later he hit a hanging curveball for a two-run homer in the sixth that produced another win over the Expos. Thus in four games, he had produced three game-winning hits.

Whatever doubts the Mets had about Shinjo when he was popping the ball up in spring training had been eliminated.

"We thought he was going to amount to a very good fourth outfielder, a pinch runner, and a late-inning defensive replacement," said pitcher Al Leiter. "I don't think anyone thought he was going to be as good as he has been."

Added pitcher John Franco, "We heard a lot about him, that he was a pretty good player and a Gold Glove winner in Japan, so he had to have some talent. The question was, will he hit here? He's proven he can do it."

Valentine had urged those who were trying to judge Shinjo prematurely to be patient, and not only because he knew it would take time for the player to show his true baseball skills. He also knew there would be a definite period of transition off the field, as Shinjo learned the American culture and lifestyle.

Shinjo credited his mother and father, who is a gardener and an expert in the martial arts, for helping him develop mental toughness as a youngster. "I feel lonely still, but I need to be mentally tough,"

Shinjo said. "My parents used to be strict, so I naturally grew up with mental toughness."

Shinjo also was impressing the Mets with his ability to make adjustments not just from one at-bat to another but from one pitch to another, especially with pitchers he had never faced before.

"He's the one who's supposed to be at a disadvantage, not knowing the pitchers, but he sees one pitch and he won't be fooled by it again," said hitting coach Dave Engle.

Added Shinjo, "When they throw a curveball and I miss with the swing, I am drawing a line of the pitch [from the pitcher's hand to the catcher's mitt]. It sticks in my mind. Next time I see it, I can remember the line and hit it."

Shinjo's mere ground ball to second in the eighth inning turned into a big play on June 17 against the Yankees, and only time will tell how big a play it may turn out to be for the Mets. Hustling all the way, he was able to beat a relay from second with a twisting, turning slide. Instead of the play being an inning-ending double play, Mike Piazza got to bat, and he ripped a game-winning homer.

That play convinced the Mets that Shinjo was indeed hurt, and he was placed on the disabled list with a strained left quadriceps.

That ended a stretch in which Shinjo drove in eleven runs in a twelve-game span, all while playing on a sore leg.

"He has inspired the whole team," Valentine said.

Inspiring the team was not one of Valentine's and the Mets' expectations for Shinjo, but they will take it as an added bonus and continue pulling for him to come through with more clutch hits.

"It's difficult for me to relate to him," said first baseman Todd Zeile. "He's completely alone. He's trying to be a pioneer, and every pioneer takes risks. I'm pulling for him."

Shinjo's early success with the Mets might have been surprising to some, but at least he had a track record in Japan to fall back on. When another of the Japanese players currently in the major leagues, pitcher Mac Suzuki, came to the United States in the spring of 1992, he was sixteen years old and should have been in high school.

Mac Suzuki was a true pioneer when he moved from Japan to join an independent Class A team in the California League, crossing the Pacific Ocean before he ever had pitched in a professional game in Japan.

He had gotten kicked out of high school for fighting, and his parents decided it would be good for him to leave Japan and begin working. Don Nomura, who later became an agent for Japanese players, was a part owner of the team in Salinas, California, and he told Suzuki he would give him a job. Nomura had first met Suzuki in 1990 when the young man attended a baseball camp Nomura was running in San Diego.

"I was a little wild as a kid, and they [his parents] made the decision because they thought it would be a good thing for me," Suzuki said.

Suzuki thought he was going to be a pitcher, but he also knew part of the arrangement was that when he wasn't pitching, he would be working at the stadium. He understood his job would be in the concession stand, selling hot dogs and the like.

That wasn't exactly the way it turned out, however.

When he showed up for his first day of work, there was no uniform for him. He was told his job was to clean up the old stadium, moving a lot of boxes.

"I was thinking this isn't baseball, this isn't pitching," Suzuki said. "But I also thought it was still ten days before the season started, and maybe this is what the players did before the season started. But then the season started, and I had the same job."

Suzuki was the team's "clubbie," meaning it was his job to make sure the locker room was clean and that all of the laundry was done. He was making $300 a month.

One of the hardest parts of his job was trying to communicate with the players, because he didn't know any English and none of them knew any Japanese.

"Every day somebody was always missing something like a sock or a T-shirt, and players were yelling at me in English 'where's my sock' and I didn't understand. I got in a lot of fights."

Suzuki's normal work day began at 7 A.M. or 8 A.M., and he often didn't finish until 2 A.M. or 3 A.M. the following morning. He lived in the clubhouse that summer, usually sleeping on a couch or the table in the trainer's room when he had a chance.

Because it was an independent team, there was no pipeline of players from a major league organization, and the team was bad. It finished the year with a record of 36 and 99, a whopping 45½ games out of first place.

Suzuki kept asking Nomura when he was going to get a chance to pitch. Finally, on the last day of the season, he was able to make his professional debut with one scoreless inning in relief.

Nomura sold the team after that season, and Suzuki was guaranteed a roster spot with an independent team in San Bernadino after Nomura told team officials he was twenty, not seventeen. He pitched in forty-eight games, going 4 and 4 with twelve saves, and was ranked as the sixth best prospect in the league by *Baseball America*.

"I had a good arm, but I didn't pitch well," he said. "I was wild."

He and Nomura, now his agent, received offers from fifteen organizations before deciding to sign with Seattle. Suzuki was invited to the major league spring training camp, where Japanese reporters began to follow his progress closely. It was headline news when former AL batting champion Edgar Martinez broke his bat while hitting against Suzuki in batting practice.

He also showed his sense of humor by asking for uniform number 911, after he asked Seattle farm director Jim Beattie what telephone number Americans call in case of emergency. He finally settled for number 96, the highest recording his fastball had registered on the radar gun.

The Mariners were excited about his potential—this was still a year before Hideo Nomo was to make his debut with the Dodgers.

"Hell, if he made our team and did pretty good, there's no telling what it could mean," said Seattle pitching coach Sammy Ellis. "We might end up with a Japanese cable television contract."

Said manager Lou Piniella, "He's a good-looking young pitcher. I was impressed with his work habits, with his coachability and his poise. He has great ability. The one thing we did not see was that 95 mph he promises."

Part of the reason for that might have been that Suzuki was starting to have arm problems. He developed tendonitis in his right shoulder and elbow and would pitch in only eighteen games over the 1994 and 1995 seasons. He eventually underwent surgery on his shoulder.

While he was hurt in 1995, he had to watch all of the attention Hideo Nomo was receiving as a rookie with the Dodgers. Suzuki didn't know Nomo and in a way resented him for getting so much notoriety.

"I shouldn't have been jealous, and I had no reason to be jealous of him," Suzuki said. "I had only pitched good in A ball and I was hurt and on the DL; still I was jealous of him."

Suzuki was determined to keep working, however, and began the 1996 season in Double A. He was called up to the Mariners on July 4 and made his major league debut against Texas on July 7, becoming the first Japanese-born pitcher in American League history. After pitching a scoreless sixth inning, he got one out in the seventh but was charged with three runs. He was optioned back to the minors four days later and finished the year at Triple A Tacoma.

Part of the key to his success was getting to know and spend time working out during the winter with Nomo, who also was represented by Nomura.

"I got a chance to talk with him and I learned a lot from him," said Suzuki, no longer jealous. "He knew a lot, especially about baseball. He helped me a lot."

Suzuki began to put that knowledge to work in 1997, when he spent the entire year at Triple A Tacoma. He was back at Tacoma in 1998, working primarily as a starter, and was called up again by the Mariners in September.

He made his first major league start on September 2 at Boston and picked up his first major league win on September 14 at Minnesota, when he struck out a career-high eight batters in 6⅓ innings. One of his starts that month was against the Yankees' Hideki Irabu, the first matchup ever in the majors between Japanese starters.

At the age of twenty-three, Suzuki figured to just be coming into his prime, but instead his Mariners' career was about to end. He split his time between starting and relieving in the first two months of the 1999 season, but on June 18 he was traded to the New York Mets for pitcher Allen Watson.

The Mets placed Suzuki on waivers almost immediately, and he was claimed by the Royals on June 22.

"Seattle gave me a lot of opportunities," Suzuki said. "I couldn't win."

The Royals were hoping a fresh start in a new organization would help unleash Suzuki's potential. He divided his time between starting and relieving for Kansas City in the second half of the 1999 season, then moved into the rotation in 2000.

He even started Kansas City's home opener against Minnesota, allowing four runs and six hits in 4½ innings in a game the Royals eventually won 10 to 6.

By the end of the year, Suzuki was Kansas

City's best starter. He entered September with a record of 8 and 7 and a 3.93 ERA, but once again he was hampered by a sore shoulder. He went 0 and 3 in the final month and underwent shoulder surgery again in October.

Again he came back quicker than expected and was back in Kansas City's rotation in April 2001. His teammates were not surprised by how quickly Suzuki was able to pitch again, knowing how hard he was worked at every level of his career. That skill was probably first instilled in him by his parents, who had him begin taking karate lessons when he was three years old. By age fourteen, he was a second-degree black belt.

"He taught me a little karate last year but I had to quit because he practices a little too hard, he was hurting me," pitcher Jeff Suppan told the *Kansas City Star*. "I'd say, 'Mac, can't you take it easy on me?' And he said, 'No, you've got to practice hard.' That shows you he's a very determined person. I think he has a high pain tolerance. He's going to be healthy this season, he's going to be ready."

The Royals' biggest concern with Suzuki was the number of pitches he throws in a game, which is always high because of his control problems. He led the team with 135 strikeouts in 2000 but also led the staff with ninety-four walks in 188 innings.

By the end of April, six months after his surgery, Suzuki was pitching and pitching well. He worked eight shutout innings on April 26 to raise his record to 2 and 1 and lower his ERA to 2.16.

The consistency that the Royals had hoped Suzuki would find never came, however, and their need for a veteran catcher forced them to include Suzuki in a trade to Colorado on June 24 for Brent Mayne.

In July he was placed on waivers by Colorado and claimed by Milwaukee. Despite his long career, he still is only twenty-six years old.

Despite all of the ups and downs in his career, Suzuki has never thought about quitting, except for the first few days of his job as a "clubbie" in Salinas in 1992. All the while, he has continued to watch more and more Japanese players come to the major leagues and perform well.

One of those was Hideki Irabu, whom many people predicted would be more successful than Nomo when he left Japan in 1997.

At least one American coaching in Japan when Hideki Irabu was pitching for Chiba Lotte called him the Nolan Ryan of Japan. Tom House, the pitching coach for Chiba Lotte, also said he had seen Irabu "throw probably 20 pitches over 100 mph."

Whether House was guilty of exaggeration or not, when it became clear that Irabu was ready to leave Japan for the major leagues after the 1996 season, a number of teams were interested.

Irabu led the Japanese Pacific League in ERA in

1995 and 1996, led the league in strikeouts in 1994 and 1995, and led the league in wins (fifteen) in 1994. At the age of twenty-seven the right-hander appeared headed for the prime years of his career.

Bobby Valentine had managed Irabu for the Marines and wanted him to join him with the Mets. The Yankees wanted to sign him, sending their director of international scouting, Gordon Blakeley, to Japan to watch him pitch. The Padres also were very interested.

The problem with signing Irabu was that unlike Nomo, the Chiba Lotte team was not willing to release him from his contract and he had not reached the ten-year service requirement before reaching free agency. The commissioner's office issued a fax to all clubs in December 1996 advising them that there were to be no negotiations with Irabu or his agent, Nomura, until he had been released by Chiba Lotte.

The Mets thought they had an agreement with Chiba Lotte, in which they basically would trade players and send cash to the Marines for the rights to Irabu. The Padres actually did sign a working agreement with the Marines, calling for a yearly exchange of players and giving them the exclusive rights to sign Irabu. Despite this, the Yankees weren't about to give up.

Nomura reported that Irabu only wanted to pitch for the Yankees and threatened to skip the 1997 season unless Chiba Lotte worked out a deal with that team. The dispute eventually went to a hearing ordered by the commissioner's office, with Irabu and Nomura arguing that he should become a free agent, free to negotiate with all major league clubs, and the Padres arguing that they had obtained his exclusive rights to him.

It was a delicate issue. Not only did officials of Major League Baseball have to worry about relationships among their own clubs, but they knew their ruling could have a definite impact on the Japan league as well. The relationship with Japanese teams was important to the major leagues, and they didn't want this dispute to tarnish years of goodwill between the two countries.

After the hearing the Executive Council ruled that the Padres owned the exclusive negotiating rights to Irabu and would lose them only if his former Japanese team withdrew those rights.

Any other ruling would definitely have not been received well by the Japanese, said Padres consultant Dan Okimoto.

"To argue that Irabu should be a free agent is absolutely absurd," Okimoto told the *San Diego Union Tribune*. "This is the petty, narrow, parochial self-interest of George Steinbrenner and the New York Yankees, and it basically says to hell with everything, to hell with the Japanese, to hell with the internationalization of baseball. 'We want this player, he should be a free agent.' "

Irabu and Nomura were upset by the ruling but had little recourse except to begin negotiations with the Padres. Those negotiations, however, included a new twist—a demand to be traded to the Yankees before he would agree to sign.

The Padres and others in baseball had to wonder if all of this fuss was really worth it. Was Irabu that good?

Irabu's father was a U.S. serviceman stationed in Okinawa. Raised in Osaka, Irabu was recruited out of junior high to play baseball for one of the best high school teams in the country. He grew to be a big star, including physically, at 6 foot 5 and 230 pounds.

He also was known for having temper outbursts. When he lost a game for the Marines because of a ninth-inning home run that wrapped around the foul pole, he showed up the next day with a broken toe—the result of kicking something in anger.

When he wasn't losing his temper, however, Irabu was displaying Nolan Ryan–like ability.

"He does remind me of Nolan, especially with the way he finishes his pitch, out front of the release point," House told the *Union-Tribune*. "He's a big kid who physically does some of the same things Nolan does. You can see that just watching him play catch."

Former major leaguer Tom O'Malley faced Irabu often in Japan.

"He's the real deal," O'Malley told the *New*

York Daily News. "He throws his fastball in the upper 90s and he throws his forkball in the low 90s, a hard forkball like Mike Scott threw. I think he'd do well here as a No. 1 or 2 starter. Hideo Nomo's a good pitcher, but this guy's a great pitcher.

"Last time I faced him was in an All-Star game last year. He struck me out 1-2-3. . . . He's got the arm of a young Nolan Ryan. He's certainly not as polished, but he has that kind of potential."

One San Diego columnist likened the dispute between major league baseball and Irabu to "a mother trying to get her child to eat spinach."

Nomura maintained that Irabu would pitch only for the Yankees, despite baseball's ruling. "He will not be a Padre," Nomura said. "He will never wear their uniform."

At least seven teams, including the Yankees, contacted the Padres about a possible trade for Irabu, but the Padres refused to change their position. Nomura further angered San Diego officials by claiming that the Padres were treating Irabu like he was a prisoner.

"Mr. Irabu is being kept against his will, as if he were a prisoner," Nomura said. "He is being held hostage to the special interests of baseball."

The dispute dragged on throughout spring training. Finally, in April, the Padres gave in and traded Irabu's rights along with three minor leaguers to the Yankees for outfielder Ruben Rivera, right-handed pitcher Rafael Medina, and $3 million.

"I'm sure everyone is glad it's over," said San Diego general manager Kevin Towers.

San Diego newspaper columnists had a field day with the story. "I didn't know that it's possible to rid yourself of something you've never had, but the Padres have done it, and it is a good riddance, sorry to say," wrote Nick Canepa in the *Union-Tribune*. "In a way, I'm more than angry about this, because the crumb got what he wanted, or what his agent, Don Nomura, wanted. They didn't play by the rules and ended up getting it their way. And so did the Yankees, who lost the battle but whined and cried and manipulated until they received a surrender, which they expected all along, because they are the Yankees."

Another month later Irabu finally agreed to a four-year, $12.8 million contract with the Yankees.

New York officials almost fell over themselves trying to slap each other on the back when Irabu finally made his U.S. debut in May, pitching four innings for Class A Tampa against the St. Lucie Mets in a Florida State League game.

He allowed one hit and struck out six of the thirteen batters he faced. "This kid is the real deal," said former major leaguer and Tampa manager Lee Mazzilli. "I think what you saw was just the tip of the iceberg. This kid has a lot going for him."

After a month in the minor leagues, Irabu joined

the Yankees and made his major league debut on July 10 against Detroit. He pitched 6⅔ innings, allowing two runs on five hits while striking out nine. He earned a curtain call from the fans at Yankee Stadium after going into the dugout.

Unfortunately for Irabu and the Yankees, the film of his highlights in New York didn't last very long. Less than three weeks later, he was back in the minor leagues. He was recalled in August but finished the year with a 5 and 4 record and a 7.09 ERA. The Yankees took part of the blame for his poor season, admitting they rushed him after the prolonged contract negotiations.

His 1998 season didn't begin much better. Upset when a Japanese cameraman refused to stop filming what Irabu thought was an off-the-record discussion, Irabu stepped on the cameraman's foot and almost broke his $60,000 camera. He continued to feud with the Japanese media all year, no matter whether he was pitching well or during stretches when he was struggling.

In June he was 6 and 2 and leading the American League with a 1.68 ERA. By September he had lost four of six decisions, and his ERA was threatening to surpass 4.00. Owner George Steinbrenner said he was not giving up on Irabu but was closely monitoring his performance.

"He knows I've been disappointed," Steinbrenner told the *New York Daily News*. "I don't think he's the kind of guy who likes to let people down.

His numbers are still pretty damn good and he's a good pitcher. He's worked hard all year, so I am not giving up on him."

Despite his thirteen wins for the season, he didn't pitch in the playoffs or World Series. When he reported to spring training the following year, the Yankees weren't sure what to expect.

In a game against the Phillies, he failed to cover first base on a grounder to the right side and drew the ire of pitching coach Mel Stottlemyre and others. "It's hard for me sometimes to get inside his head and see where he is," Stottlemyre said.

Matters got worse only a few days later, in his next start of the spring, when Irabu again failed to cover first base. This time Steinbrenner spoke out.

"He looks like a fat toad out there, not covering first base," Steinbrenner said. "I don't know what you've got to do. That's not a Yankee."

When the Yankees broke camp and prepared to begin the regular season, Irabu was left behind.

"It's not a slap on the wrist, it's just a decision I made, whether it's right or wrong," Steinbrenner said. "I saw some very good things that he did out there. I reacted when I made those statements. He is overweight and we have to get his weight down."

Irabu rejoined the team a few days later and apologized to his teammates but still failed to find the command of his pitches that he had been used to in Japan. His inconsistency was the most troubling part of his performance for manager Joe

Torre, who had no idea what to expect from game to game.

Seemingly for every game like a three-hit shut-out over Detroit, there was a game in which he was hit hard. By August, however, it appeared that Irabu had found the consistency he had been missing. He won eight consecutive decisions, to improve his record to 9 to 3, and was the pitcher of the month for July in the American League. By September, however, he was struggling again, and went from being a lock to be in the Yankees' rotation in the playoffs to being left off the roster for the World Series.

Irabu admitted he was disappointed by the season when he finished 11 and 7.

"I feel like I left a lot of things undone that I wanted to do, things I didn't finish on the field," he said through an interpreter. "I don't think right now is the time for me to think about next year."

What Irabu didn't know at the time was that next year, he would no longer be a Yankee. In December he was traded to Montreal for three minor league pitchers. After all of that fuss with the Padres, Irabu's Yankee career totaled a mere seventy-four games, for a 29 and 20 record.

"Maybe he'll get a chance to start fresh in a new league," said Yankees' general manager Brian Cashman. "He was always under a microscope here. Maybe he can get away from the expectations he had on him here. New York is a tough situation. It's not for everybody."

Unfortunately for Irabu, the move to Montreal didn't produce much better results. He was the No. 2 starter in the Expos' rotation leaving spring training in 1999 but then saw his season shortened because of two operations, one on his knee and one on his elbow. He made only eleven starts in the majors, winning twice.

He began the 2001 season on the disabled list, and in his third start on June 13, he found himself back in Yankee Stadium. "I have kind of mixed feelings," he said. "But I'm very happy to pitch."

The *Montreal Gazette* reported that Yankee fans pretty much treated Irabu as they would any tourist, by ignoring him, but the Yankees roughed up their former teammate with a 9 to 3 victory.

Nine days later, it was revealed that Irabu had a partial tear in his right elbow and perhaps would have to undergo season-ending surgery. For a pitcher who had been so promising only five years earlier that he was called the Japanese Nolan Ryan, this was just the latest frustrating setback in a career of disappointments.

When Irabu was making his stormy and demanding entrance to the majors in 1997, another pitcher was very quietly settling in with the California Angels. Shigetoshi Hasegawa has been there ever since.

———

While Irabu's contract dispute was headline news for weeks, the announcement that the Anaheim Angels had signed Shigetoshi Hasegawa was condensed to a one-paragraph story in a roundup of sports briefs in the *Los Angeles Times*.

Hasegawa had pitched six years for Orix, where he was a teammate of Ichiro, and proved to be very dependable and consistent. He was 53 and 39 in Japan with a 3.11 ERA. Scouts said he was more of a finesse than a power pitcher, relying on pinpoint control and an assortment of breaking balls and off-speed pitches to be effective. He was the Pacific League's Rookie of the Year in 1991 when he was 12 and 9, but that turned out to be the most games he would win in a season, although he twice matched that total.

He learned baseball from his grandfather, who was a grade school coach and a catcher in baseball and softball leagues in Japan. Hasegawa's grandfather also emphasized the importance of locating his pitches, especially if he was not an overpowering pitcher.

Hasegawa listened well, and he tried always to follow his grandfather's advice. He also knew coming to the United States that he wanted the experience to be fun, getting away from some of the regimentation that is so common in Japan.

Once in the United States, he quickly showed he had a sense of humor, saying he signed with the Angels because the team was owned by the Walt

Disney Company. "The pitcher is Mickey Mouse and the catcher is Minnie Mouse," he said.

The Angels were not expecting the twenty-eight-year-old Hasegawa to take the major leagues by storm. They were hoping he would prove to be a quality relief pitcher, and that's exactly what he turned out to be.

Hasegawa admitted he was a little worried in his first spring training appearance, when the first batter he was called on to face was Barry Bonds.

"I looked at him and thought, 'My timing is not very good,' " Hasegawa said. "It was a big surprise. He's a problem for me."

He wasn't in this game. Bonds lined out to second, and Hasegawa retired the Giants in order. In his next inning, however, he gave up back-to-back doubles and the Angels went on to lose the game.

Quickly nicknamed "Shaggy," by his teammates, Hasegawa also had to face an onslaught of Japanese media, but he did not have any of the problems Nomo and Irabu had experienced. He told both the Japanese and American reporters that he learned English by watching the movie *Field of Dreams*—twelve times.

He became a favorite of his new teammates and proved he could dish out abuse as easily as he could take it. Some teammates tried to help him learn English, but they added a few choice words along the way.

"That's OK," Hasegawa told the *Los Angeles*

Times. "I appreciate them doing that because I learned what those words mean. If someone from another team says them to me in a game, I know I should get mad."

When he made his regular season debut by starting the Angels' game on April 5 against Cleveland, the game was televised live back to Japan.

"I'm excited but a little bit nervous," Hasegawa said. "I know the reputation of the new players Cleveland has. They're a great hitting team."

Hasegawa quickly downplayed any comparisons to Nomo, pitching up the freeway for the Dodgers.

"There's no pressure on me to be like him because our styles are completely different," he said. "How he [Nomo] does is of no importance to me, because he is a major league pitcher and I am not one yet. I'm trying to become one."

Hasegawa also wasn't concerned about comparisons between the major leagues and the Japanese leagues, and neither was his manager, Terry Collins. All Collins was worried about was whether the umpire was going to have a low strike zone.

"If he's not getting the low strike," Collins said of Hasegawa, "there's a chance he'll have a rough night. The thing he can't do is get frustrated because he makes a pitch that was a strike in the past but is a ball here."

His debut wasn't great, but it also wasn't a disaster. He pitched 4⅓ innings, allowing seven hits and five runs, including a homer by Sandy Alomar Jr., in a 7 to 5 loss.

Hasegawa made seven starts for the Angels as a rookie but was used mostly as a middle reliever. His first career win, on April 15 at New York, was headline news in his homeland.

Some Japanese reporters said they thought fans were more interested in following Hasegawa than Nomo for the same reasons that fans were more interested in Shinjo than Ichiro five years later. Nomo was expected to be a star, while Hasegawa was seen as more of an average pitcher.

"If Hasegawa succeeds, then a lot of pitchers here can succeed in the States," said John De Bellis, a sportswriter for the *Asahi Evening News*. "It means Japanese baseball may finally be on par with what even the Japanese call 'the major leagues.'"

That also wasn't something Hasegawa was concerned with. He wanted to be successful on his own terms, and he was very pleased when most Japanese media people found something else to keep them busy once his rookie season was over.

He also felt more comfortable on the mound, having become accustomed to facing the hitters that had given him trouble as a rookie.

"Last year, I was a little afraid of players like Frank Thomas and Ken Griffey," Hasegawa told the *Los Angeles Times*. "When I talked with Cecil Fielder this year, I found out he wasn't a monster.

Now I'm not scared of Frank Thomas or Albert Belle or Ken Griffey. They are all human, like me.

"Mark McGwire, now he's a monster. He's not human."

In 1998 Hasegawa became one of the Angels' most consistent pitchers. The lack of attention probably helped, because it took that extra distraction away and didn't single him out from his teammates.

"I don't think it [the lack of attention] has bothered him," pitcher Troy Percival told the *Los Angeles Times*. "Nothing seems to bother him. He just goes about his business. Apparently in Japan they don't see being in the bullpen as prestigious as being a starter, but the role he has played for us is as valuable as any position on this team."

Said Hasegawa, "Starting pitchers are big in Japan, really big. It is my job to explain relief pitching to the people of Japan."

So while Hasegawa was pitching very effectively for the Angels, all of the Japanese media attention was going to Nomo, Irabu, and Masato Yoshii.

"If you ask me," said the Angels' Phil Nevin, "this guy is the best of the Japanese pitchers and no one knows about him."

Hasegawa credited his improvement to knowing the hitters better than he did as a rookie and with not making as many mistakes, leaving balls over the middle of the plate that could be hammered for home runs.

He completed his second season with an 8 and 3 record, five saves, and a 3.14 ERA. That was a sign of things to come, as he led the Angels' staff in appearances in 1999. The year 2000 was the best year of his career, with Hasegawa winning ten games and saving nine.

During one stretch of the season, from July 13 to August 29, he pitched 27½ consecutive scoreless innings. He also did not allow an inherited runner to score for thirty-five consecutive innings.

His ten wins were the most on the Angels' staff. He also proved effective in the closer's role when filling in for the injured Percivel.

Pitching coach Bud Black was impressed.

"What makes a relief pitcher reliable and functional is his ability to be resilient," Black told the *Los Angeles Times*. "It is the ability to come ready to pitch every day, both mentally and physically. He has those qualities."

Hasegawa's workload might have caught up with him in 2001, when he suffered a partial tear in his right rotator cuff that forced him onto the disabled list. He thinks he was hurt partly because of his workload during his years in Japan and the fact that Japanese teams don't use specialized strength and flexibility exercises.

"I've got to tell the Japanese people that's too much," Hasegawa told the *Times*. "I don't want to see Japanese pitchers come over to the U.S. and, after a year, everybody is done."

Coming to the United States proved to be everything he thought it would be for Hasegawa, who even wrote a book titled *Adjustment* about adapting to baseball and life in this country.

Another pitcher who did that, after a long career in Japan, was Masato Yoshii.

It was surprising for a variety of reasons when Masato Yoshii decided to leave Japan and jump to the major leagues in 1998. He already had pitched thirteen years in the Japanese League, would celebrate his thirty-third birthday only three weeks into the 1998 season, and turned down at least one more lucrative offer to remain in Japan.

Still, after having pitched ten years for the Kintetsu Buffaloes and three years with the Yakult Swallows, he decided the time was right and signed with the New York Mets. He immediately moved into a spot in the New York starting rotation, but as he prepared for his first game, even general manager Steve Phillips said he had no idea what to expect.

"It should be interesting to see," Phillips said. "And I don't know that what happens [today] will be indicative of the future."

That was especially true since Yoshii had been a reliever for much of his career in Japan.

"I had to situate myself to the conditions," he

said through an interpreter. "I can very easily focus now. If you think about things all the time, you'll never sleep as a reliever."

What helped Yoshii prepare was staying up all night in Japan whenever possible to watch games Hideo Nomo pitched. All were televised live, and if Yoshii was pitching the next day, he would tape the game and watch it later.

Yoshii didn't know how many people in his homeland would be up at 2:30 A.M. to watch his debut against the Pirates, but if they weren't, they missed a good game. He pitched seven shutout innings, striking out seven batters. He later added another seven innings before finally allowing his first earned run in the majors.

He went on to enjoy a solid rookie season with the Mets, going 6 and 8 with a 3.93 ERA in twenty-nine starts, posting nine no-decisions in a stretch of fourteen starts between May and August.

Yoshii's second year with the Mets was even better. He won twelve games and at the end of the year was the team's best pitcher. In his last ten starts he was 5 and 1 with a 1.74 ERA, and he started three more games in the playoffs.

Because of that success, it was somewhat surprising when the Mets traded Yoshii during the off-season to the Colorado Rockies for two younger pitchers. Phillips said Yoshii still figured to be the fifth starter in the New York rotation, and, with his salary of $3 million, he became the most vulnerable person to deal.

Yoshii's year in Colorado was a struggle. He lost fifteen games but, surprisingly, was hit harder on the road, losing twelve away games, than he was at Coors Field. When it didn't appear he would make the Rockies opening day roster in 2001, he was given his release during spring training.

After contacting several clubs, Yoshii signed as a free agent with the Montreal Expos. The move reunited him with fellow Japanese pitcher Hideki Irabu and made both of them feel a little more at home.

"It's nice to have someone to speak Japanese with," Yoshii said.

With more and more Japanese players moving to the major leagues, and even more expected to come in the future, that will continue to become easier and easier. The future likely will include more players such as right-handed pitcher Tomokazu Ohka, a twenty-five-year-old who made his debut for the Red Sox in 1999 and has been up and down between the majors and minors for the past three seasons.

He showed his potential by pitching only the third perfect game in the 117-year history of the Triple A International League in 2000, a 2 to 0 gem for Pawtucket over Charlotte on June 1. He was the Boston organization's minor league pitcher of the

year in 1999, when he had a perfect 15 and 0 record
in combined stops and Double A and Triple A. He
was the starting pitcher in the home opener for the
Red Sox this year.

Ohka signed with the Red Sox after spending
four years with the Yokohama Bay Stars, but he
pitched in only thirty-four games in those four
years and started only four games, posting a 1 and
2 record.

Any time a player leaves Japan to come to the
United States, there is no guarantee that he is going
to like the new cultural experience or that he is
going to be successful. Oftentimes the two go
hand-in-hand; the better the player does profession-
ally, the easier it becomes to make the cultural
adjustments necessary when living in a different
country.

Some Japanese players who have jumped to the
majors have not been successful and didn't stay
long before returning to Japan. For example, Tak-
ashi Kashiwada pitched for the Mets in 1997 but
didn't return the next year. Masao Kida spent the
1999 season with the Detroit Tigers, then pitched
in the minors in 2000 before going back to Japan.

Other players came to the United States to play
under minor league contracts, and that situation
also is likely to increase in the coming years. Some
organizations are allocating more resources to scout
Japanese high school and college programs, trying

to sign players for their clubs before they get into the professional ranks in Japan.

As with minor leaguers from any country, undoubtedly some of those players will advance to the majors and others won't.

The biggest percentage of Japanese players coming to the major leagues, however, likely will continue to be established professionals who have either reached or are close to reaching eligibility for free agency. Today three players fall into that category and have prompted the most speculation about whether they will attempt to move to the major leagues in 2002.

Left-handed pitcher Kazuhisa Ishii of the Yakult Swallows is twenty-seven and began this year with a career record of 66 and 40 and a 3.38 ERA. He won the Central League ERA title last year with a mark of 2.61, pitched a no-hitter in 1997, and led the Central League in strikeouts in 1998. He is in his tenth season in Japan.

Ray Poitevint, the international scouting director of the Red Sox, told the *Japan Times* he has seen Ishii pitch more than a dozen times. Ishii's fastball has been clocked at 97 mph.

"I certainly think he is capable of pitching in the big leagues and probably being a number 3 starter," Poitevint told the *Japan Times*. "I think his mental toughness on the mound sets up everything. I think on a given night all of his pitches are equal, which is what makes him a real competitor."

The key to Ishii's future in the major leagues might be how much money the Swallows will look to receive from a major league club before releasing him from his contract. Scouts estimate that it will cost around $5 million for Yakult to let Ishii leave.

The two position players observers say are the most likely to try to move to the major leagues share the same last name, Matsui, but are not related. Hideki Matsui is an outfielder with the Yomuri Giants and is considered one of the best power hitters in Japan. He recently hit the 250th homer of his professional career.

Kazuo Matsui is the shortstop for the Seibu Lions and reportedly one of the best base stealers in Japan. Scouts in Japan compare him to the big three American League shortstops—Derek Jeter, Alex Rodriguez, and Nomar Garciaparra. He was the Pacific League MVP in 1998 when he hit .311 with forty-three stolen bases.

A switch-hitter, Matsui was moved out of the leadoff spot into the third spot in Seibu's batting order. In 2000 Matsui hit .322 (fifth in the league) with twenty-three homers, ninety RBI, and twenty-six stolen bases.

Now twenty-five, Matsui is playing his eighth year with the Lions and has a career .305 average. Technically he would not be eligible for free agency until after the 2003 season, when he would be twenty-eight, unless he is posted early.

Hideki Matsui, on the other hand, will be eligible for free agency after the 2002 season. Ichiro was posted a year before he could become a free agent, and some observers expect the same thing to happen with Matsui.

The difference is that he plays for the Yomuri Giants, the most lucrative team in Japan, managed by Japanese legend Shigeo Nagashima.

"I don't think it will happen, that he will come to America," Hiro Ichioka, a Japanese television producer, told the *Seattle Post-Intelligencer*. "The Giants are like the Yankees there, and the manager [Nagashima] is a very charismatic figure, like Ruth or Gehrig. If he said to Matsui, 'Stay for me,' he would stay.

"But with everything that has happened with Ichiro, who can say for certain?"

PLAYER STATISTICS IN JAPAN

Ichiro Suzuki

RECORDS

- Pacific League single-season record for most hit by pitches—18 (1985)
- Shares Nippon Professional baseball single-game record for most doubles—4 (September 11, 1994)
- Nippon Professional Baseball single-season (1994) record for most (210) hits.
- Nippon Professional Baseball single-season record for most consecutive plate appearances (216) with no strikeouts (April 16–June 25, 1997)
- Shares inning record for most stolen bases—2 (July 24, 1997, ninth inning)
- Pacific league single-season record for highest batting averages—.387 (2000)
- Career record for most games batting streak—11 (July 23, 1996–July 26, 2000)
- Shares single-game record for most hits—4 (July 24, 1999, July 23, 2000)
- Shares single-game record for most long hits—3 (July 24, 1999)
- Shares single-series record for most consecutive hits—5 (July 22–23, 2000)

- Nippon Professional Baseball career record for most (7) consecutive years with league leading in batting average
- Shares Nippon Professional baseball career record for most years leading league in batting average—7

TITLES
- Pacific League RBI Leader (1995)
- Pacific league Batting Champion (1994–2000)
- Pacific League Stolen bases Leader (1995)
- Pacific League On-Base Percentage Leader (1994–96, 1999–2000)

HONORS
- Pacific League Most Valuable Player (1994–1996)
- Outfielder on Pacific League All Star Team (1994–2000)
- Pacific League Gold Glove as outfielder (1994–2000)

REGULAR SEASON

		BATTING												FIELDING		
YEAR	TEAM	G	AB	Avg	R	H	2B	3B	HR	RBI	BB	SO	SB	PO	A	E
1992	Orix Blue Wave	40	95	.253	9	24	5	0	0	5	3	11	3	50	0	0
1993	Orix Blue Wave	43	64	.188	4	12	2	0	1	3	2	7	0	34	1	5
1994	Orix Blue Wave	130	546	.385	111	210	41	5	13	54	51	53	29	261	10	2
1995	Orix Blue Wave	130	524	.342	104	179	23	4	25	80	68	52	49	262	14	2
1996	Orix Blue Wave	130	542	.356	104	193	24	4	16	84	56	57	35	277	8	2
1997	Orix Blue Wave	135	536	.345	94	185	31	4	17	91	62	36	39	269	7	3
1998	Orix Blue Wave	135	506	.358	79	181	36	3	13	71	43	35	11	245	12	3
1999	Orix Blue Wave	103	411	.343	80	141	27	2	21	68	45	46	12	196	10	0
2000	Orix Blue Wave	105	395	.387	73	153	22	1	12	73	54	36	21	218	5	4
TOTALS (9 YEARS)		951	3619	.353	658	1278	211	23	118	529	384	333	199	1812	67	18

JAPAN SERIES

		BATTING										FIELDING		
YEAR	TEAM	G	AB	Avg	R	H	2B	3B	HR	RBI	BB	SO	SB	PO	A	E
1995	Onix Blue Wave	5	19	.263	1	5	0	0	1	2	3	4	0	10	2	0
1996	Onix Blue Wave	5	19	.263	3	5	0	0	1	1	2	1	2	8	0	0
TOTALS (2 YEARS)		10	38	.263	4	10	0	0	2	3	5	5	2	18	2	0

ALL-STAR GAMES

RECORDS: Holds career record for most games batting streak—11 (July 23, 1996–July 26, 2000). Shares single-game record for most hits—4 (July 24, 1999, July 23, 2000). Shares single-game record for most long hits—3 (July 24, 1999). Shares single-series record for most consecutive hits—5 (July 22–23, 2000). Shares inning record for most stolen bases—2 (July 24, 1997, ninth inning).

BATTING

| | | | | | | | | | | | | | | FIELDING | | |
YEAR	LEAGUE	G	AB	Avg	R	H	2B	3B	HR	RBI	BB	SO	SB	PO	A	E
1994	Pacific League	2	10	.200	2	2	0	0	0	1	0	0	1	5	1	0
1995	Pacific League	2	10	.300	2	3	0	0	0	0	0	1	2	8	0	0
1996	Pacific League	3	10	.400	5	4	0	1	1	1	2	1	1	3	0	0
1997	Pacific League	2	9	.444	1	4	0	0	0	1	0	1	2	3	0	0
1998	Pacific League	2	8	.250	1	2	1	0	0	0	0	1	0	3	0	0
1999	Pacific League	3	13	.462	2	6	2	0	1	2	0	0	0	4	0	0
2000	Pacific League	3	11	.636	3	7	1	0	1	4	2	0	1	5	0	0
TOTALS (7 YEARS)		17	71	.394	16	28	4	1	3	9	4	4	7	31	1	0

PITCHING

YEAR	LEAGUE	W	L	G	GS	CG	ShO	Sv	IP	H	R	ER	ERA	BB	SO
1996	Pacific League	0	0	1	0	0	0	0	0.1	0	0	0	0.00	0	0
TOTALS (1 YEARS)		0	0	1	0	0	0	0	0.1	0	0	0	0.00	0	0

Shigetoshi Hasegawa

RECORDS
- Shares Pacific League single-game record for most hits allowed–19 (June 13, 1995)

HONORS
- Pacific League Rookie of the Year (1991)

REGULAR SEASON

PITCHING

YEAR	TEAM	W	L	G	GS	CG	ShO	Sv	IP	H	R	ER	ERA	BB	SO
1991	Orix Blue Wave	12	9	28	25	11	3	1	185	184	76	73	3.55	50	111
1992	Orix Blue Wave	6	8	24	19	4	0	1	143.1	138	60	52	3.27	51	86
1993	Orix Blue Wave	12	6	23	22	9	3	0	159.2	146	61	48	2.71	48	86
1994	Orix Blue Wave	11	9	25	22	8	3	1	156.1	169	61	54	3.11	46	86
1995	Orix Blue Wave	12	7	24	23	9	4	0	171	167	62	55	2.89	51	91
1996	Orix Blue Wave	4	6	18	16	2	0	1	87.2	109	60	52	5.34	40	55
TOTALS (6 YEARS)		57	45	142	127	43	13	4	903	913	380	334	3.33	286	515

YEAR	TEAM	BATTING												FIELDING		
		G	AB	Avg	R	H	2B	3B	HR	RBI	BB	SO	SB	PO	A	E
1991	Orix Blue Wave	28	0	.000	0	0	0	0	0	0	0	0	0	13	30	1
1992	Orix Blue Wave	33	0	.000	0	0	0	0	0	0	0	0	0	3	30	0
1993	Orix Blue Wave	30	0	.000	0	0	0	0	0	0	0	0	0	8	27	1
1994	Orix Blue Wave	25	0	.000	0	0	0	0	0	0	0	0	0	13	42	1
1995	Orix Blue Wave	24	0	.000	0	0	0	0	0	0	0	0	0	17	37	1
1996	Orix Blue Wave	18	0	.000	0	0	0	0	0	0	0	0	0	4	12	0
	TOTALS (6 YEARS)	158	0	.000	0	0	0	0	0	0	0	0	0	58	178	4

JAPAN SERIES

PITCHING

YEAR	TEAM	W	L	G	GS	CG	ShO	Sv	IP	H	R	ER	SB	ERA	BB	SO
1995	Orix Blue Wave	0	0	1	1	0	0	0	6	2	1	1	0	1.50	3	4
1996	Orix Blue Wave	0	0	1	0	0	0	0	2.1	1	0	0	0	0.00	0	3
TOTALS (2 YEARS)		0	0	2	1	0	0	0	8.1	3	1	1	0	1.08	3	7

BATTING

YEAR	TEAM	G	AB	Avg	R	H	2B	3B	HR	RBI	BB	SO	SB	FIELDING PO	A	E
1995	Orix Blue Wave	1	2	.000	0	0	0	0	0	0	0	0	0	0	1	0
1996	Orix Blue Wave	1	0	.000	0	0	0	0	0	0	0	0	0	0	0	0
TOTALS (2 YEARS)		2	2	.000	0	0	0	0	0	0	0	0	0	0	1	0

ALL-STAR GAMES

PITCHING

	W	L	G	S	CG	ShO	Sv	IP	H	R	ER	ERA	BB	SO
YEAR LEAGUE														
1995 Pacific League	0	0	1	0	0	0	0	2	1	1	1	4.50	0	1
TOTALS (1 YEAR)	0	0	1	0	0	0	0	2	1	1	1	4.50	0	1

FIELDING

	SB	SO	PO	A	E
1995 Pacific League	0	0	0	0	0
TOTALS (1 YEAR)	0	0	0	0	0

BATTING

	G	AB	Avg	R	H	2B	3B	HR	RBI	BB	SO
YEAR LEAGUE											
1995 Pacific League	1	0	.000	0	0	0	0	0	0	0	0
TOTALS (1 YEAR)	1	0	.000	0	0	0	0	0	0	0	0

FIELDING

	SB	SO	PO	A	E
1995 Pacific League	0	0	0	0	0
TOTALS (1 YEAR)	0	0	0	0	0

Hideki Irabu

RECORDS
- Shares Nippon Professional Baseball single-inning record for most wild pitches—3 (September 28, 1994, first inning)

TITLES
- Pacific League Strikeout leader (1994–95)
- Pacific League ERA Leader (1995–1996)

REGULAR SEASON

PITCHING

YEAR	TEAM	W	L	G	S	CG	ShO	Sv	IP	H	R	ER	ERA	BB	SO
1988	Lotte Orions	2	5	14	6	0	0	1	39.1	30	19	17	3.89	18	21
1989	Lotte Orions	0	2	33	2	0	0	9	51	37	20	20	3.53	27	50
1990	Lotte Orions	8	5	34	11	4	0	0	123.2	110	58	52	3.78	72	102
1991	Lotte Orions	3	8	24	16	2	0	0	100.2	110	78	77	6.88	70	78
1992	Chiba Lotte Marines	0	5	28	4	0	0	0	77	78	38	33	3.86	37	55
1993	Chiba Lotte Marines	8	7	32	14	6	0	1	142.1	125	59	49	3.10	58	160
1994	Chiba Lotte Marines	15	10	27	26	16	1	0	207.1	170	77	70	3.04	94	239
1995	Chiba Lotte Marines	11	11	28	27	9	2	0	203	156	70	57	2.53	72	239
1996	Chiba Lotte Marines	12	6	23	23	3	0	0	157.1	108	56	42	2.40	59	167
	TOTALS (9 YEARS)	59	59	243	129	40	3	11	1101.2	924	475	417	3.41	507	1111

		BATTING													FIELDING		
YEAR	TEAM	G	AB	Avg	R	H	2B	3B	HR	RBI	BB	SO	SB	PO	A	E
1988	Lotte Orions	27	0	.000	0	0	0	0	0	0	0	0	0	0	3	0
1989	Lotte Orions	33	0	.000	0	0	0	0	0	0	0	0	0	3	12	0
1990	Lotte Orions	36	0	.000	0	0	0	0	0	0	0	0	0	5	19	1
1991	Lotte Orions	30	0	.000	0	0	0	0	0	0	0	0	0	2	17	1
1992	Chiba Lotte Marines	32	0	.000	0	0	0	0	0	0	0	0	0	2	21	2
1993	Chiba Lotte Marines	42	0	.000	0	0	0	0	0	0	0	0	0	4	13	1
1994	Chiba Lotte Marines	27	0	.000	0	0	0	0	0	0	0	0	0	10	26	2
1995	Chiba Lotte Marines	28	0	.000	0	0	0	0	0	0	0	0	0	6	34	4
1996	Chiba Lotte Marines	23	0	.000	0	0	0	0	0	0	0	0	0	7	19	2
	TOTALS (9 YEARS)	278	0	.000	0	0	0	0	0	0	0	0	0	39	164	13

ALL-STAR GAMES

PITCHING

YEAR	LEAGUE	W	L	G	S	CG	ShO	Sv	IP	H	R	ER	ERA	BB	SO
1994	Pacific League	1	0	1	1	0	0	0	3	1	0	0	0.00	1	3
1995	Pacific League	0	1	1	0	0	0	0	2	3	3	3	13.50	2	2
1996	Pacific League	0	0	1	1	0	0	0	3	0	0	0	0.00	0	5
TOTALS (3 YEARS)		1	1	3	2	0	0	0	8	4	3	3	3.38	3	10

BATTING

YEAR	LEAGUE	G	AB	Avg	R	H	2B	3B	HR	RBI	BB	SO	SB	FIELDING PO	A	E
1994	Pacific League	1	0	.000	0	0	0	0	0	0	0	0	0	0	0	0
1995	Pacific League	1	0	.000	0	0	0	0	0	0	0	0	0	0	0	0
1996	Pacific League	1	0	.000	0	0	0	0	0	0	0	0	0	0	0	0
TOTALS (3 YEARS)		3	0	.000	0	0	0	0	0	0	0	0	0	0	0	0

Hideo Nomo

RECORDS
- Shares Nippon Professional Baseball record for most consecutive bases on balls in one inning—5 (July 10 1992, fifth inning)
- Pacific League single-season record for most bases on balls—148 (1993)
- Nippon professional Baseball single-game record for most bases on balls—16 (July 1, 1994)
- Shares Pacific League career record for most years leading league in games won—4

TITLES
- Pacific League ERA Leader (1990)
- Pacific League Winning Percentage Leader (1990)
- Pacific League Games Won Leader (1990–1993)
- Pacific League Strike-out Leader (1990–93)

HONORS
- Pacific League Most Valuable player (1990)
- Pacific League Rookie of the year (1990)

- Pitcher on Pacific League All-Star team (1990)
- Sawamura-Eiji-Sho (meaning "Japanese Cy Young Award") winner (1990)

REGULAR SEASON

PITCHING

YEAR	TEAM	W	L	G	GS	CG	ShO	Sv	IP	H	R	ER	ERA	BB	SO
1990	Kintetsu Buffaloes	18	8	29	27	21	2	0	235	167	87	76	2.91	109	287
1991	Kintetsu Buffaloes	17	11	31	29	22	4	1	242.1	183	92	82	3.05	128	287
1992	Kintetsu Buffaloes	18	8	30	29	17	5	0	216.2	150	73	64	2.66	117	228
1993	Kintetsu Buffaloes	17	12	32	32	14	2	0	243.1	201	106	100	3.70	148	276
1994	Kintetsu Buffaloes	8	7	17	17	6	0	0	114	96	55	46	3.63	86	126
TOTALS (5 YEARS)		78	46	139	134	80	13	1	1051.1	797	413	368	3.15	588	1204

BATTING

YEAR	TEAM	G	AB	Avg	R	H	2B	3B	HR	RBI	BB	SO	SB	FIELDING		
														PO	A	E
1990	Kintetsu Buffaloes	29	0	.000	0	0	0	0	0	0	0	0	0	4	22	1
1991	Kintetsu Buffaloes	31	0	.000	0	0	0	0	0	0	0	0	0	9	36	1
1992	Kintetsu Buffaloes	30	0	.000	0	0	0	0	0	0	0	0	0	10	34	0
1993	Kintetsu Buffaloes	32	0	.000	0	0	0	0	0	0	0	0	0	13	19	2
1994	Kintetsu Buffaloes	17	0	.000	0	0	0	0	0	0	0	0	0	2	12	2
TOTALS (5 YEARS)		139	0	.000	0	0	0	0	0	0	0	0	0	38	123	6

ALL-STAR GAMES

PITCHING

YEAR	LEAGUE	W	L	G	GS	CG	ShO	Sv	IP	H	R	ER	ERA	BB	SO
1990	Pacific League	0	0	2	1	0	0	0	3.1	3	2	2	5.40	3	3
1991	Pacific League	0	1	1	1	0	0	0	3	4	1	1	3.00	2	6
1992	Pacific League	0	0	1	1	0	0	0	3	2	0	0	0.00	1	5
1993	Pacific League	0	0	1	1	0	0	0	2	5	3	3	13.50	3	4
1994	Pacific League	0	0	1	0	0	0	0	0.1	0	0	0	0.00	3	1
TOTALS (5 YEARS)		0	1	6	4	0	0	0	11.2	14	6	6	4.63	12	19

BATTING

YEAR	LEAGUE	G	AB	Avg	R	H	2B	3B	HR	RBI	BB	SO	SB	PO	A	E
														FIELDING		
1990	Pacific League	2	0	.000	0	0	0	0	0	0	0	0	0	0	0	0
1991	Pacific League	2	0	.000	0	0	0	0	0	0	0	0	0	0	0	0
1992	Pacific League	1	1	.000	0	0	0	0	0	0	0	1	0	1	0	0
1993	Pacific League	1	0	.000	0	0	0	0	0	0	0	0	0	0	0	0
1994	Pacific League	1	0	.000	0	0	0	0	0	0	0	0	0	0	0	0
TOTALS (5 YEARS)		7	1	.000	0	0	0	0	0	0	0	1	0	1	0	0

Tomokazu Oka

REGULAR SEASON

YEAR	TEAM	PITCHING															
		W	L	G	GS	CG	ShO	Sv	IP	H	R	ER	ERA	BB	SO
1994	Yokohama Bay Stars	1	1	15	2	0	0	0	28	29	13	13	4.18	18	18
1995	Yokohama Bay Stars	0	0	3	1	0	0	0	9.1	3	2	2	1.93	13	6
1996	Yokohama Bay Stars	0	1	14	1	0	0	0	18	27	19	19	9.50	14	11
1998	Yokohama Bay Stars	0	0	2	0	0	0	0	2	2	2	2	9.00	2	1
TOTALS (4 YEARS)		1	2	34	4	0	0	0	57.1	61	36	36	5.65	47	36

YEAR	TEAM	BATTING												FIELDING		
		G	AB	Avg	R	H	2B	3B	HR	RBI	BB	SO	SB	PO	A	E
1994	Yokohama Bay Stars	17	3	.000	0	0	0	0	0	0	0	2	0	0	2	0
1995	Yokohama Bay Stars	4	2	.000	0	0	0	0	0	0	0	1	0	1	1	0
1996	Yokohama Bay Stars	14	1	.000	0	0	0	0	0	0	0	1	0	1	4	2
1998	Yokohama Bay Stars	2	0	.000	0	0	0	0	0	0	0	0	0	0	0	0
TOTALS (4 YEARS)		37	6	.000	0	0	0	0	0	0	0	4	0	2	7	2

Kazuhiro Sasaki

RECORDS
- Nippon Professional Baseball career record for most saves–229
- Nippon Professional Baseball single-season record for most saves–45 (1998)
- Nippon Professional Baseball single-season record for most consecutive games (22) with saves (April 26–June 30, 1998)
- Nippon Professional Baseball career record for most save-points–46 (1998)
- Nippon Professional Baseball record for most consecutive games (22) with save-points (April 26-June 30)

TITLES
- C.L. "Fireman of the Year" (1992, 1995–98)

HONORS
- C.L. Most Valuable Player (1998)
- Pitcher on C.L. All-Star team (1998)

REGULAR SEASON

PITCHING

YEAR	TEAM	W	L	G	GS	CG	ShO	Sv	IP	H	R	ER	ERA	BB	SO
1990	Yokohama Taiyo Whales	2	4	16	7	0	0	2	47.2	49	31	31	5.85	30	44
1991	Yokohama Taiyo Whales	6	9	58	1	0	0	17	117	72	33	26	2.00	51	137
1992	Yokohama Taiyo Whales	12	6	53	0	0	0	21	87.2	47	32	24	2.46	39	135
1993	Yokohama Bay Stars	3	6	38	0	0	0	20	55	35	24	20	3.27	21	84
1994	Yokohama Bay Stars	3	1	31	0	0	0	10	46	27	11	11	2.15	15	59
1995	Yokohama Bay Stars	7	2	47	0	0	0	32	56.2	30	12	11	1.75	17	78
1996	Yokohama Bay Stars	4	3	39	0	0	0	25	49.2	37	17	16	2.90	16	80
1997	Yokohama Bay Stars	3	0	49	0	0	0	38	60	25	6	6	0.90	17	99
1998	Yokohama Bay Stars	1	1	51	0	0	0	45	56	32	7	4	0.64	13	78
1999	Yokohama Bay Stars	1	1	23	0	0	0	19	23.1	19	5	5	1.93	6	34
TOTALS (10 YEARS)		42	33	405	8	0	0	229	599	373	178	154	2.31	225	828

YEAR	TEAM	BATTING												FIELDING		
		G	AB	Avg	R	H	2B	3B	HR	RBI	BB	SO	SB	PO	A	E
1990	Yokohama Taiyo Whales	25	15	.200	0	3	1	0	0	0	0	5	0	0	4	0
1991	Yokohama Taiyo Whales	58	23	.130	2	3	0	0	0	1	2	7	0	7	18	1
1992	Yokohama Taiyo Whales	53	13	.154	0	2	0	0	0	2	0	7	0	3	9	1
1993	Yokohama Bay Stars	39	9	.222	0	2	1	0	0	0	1	5	0	2	9	2
1994	Yokohama Bay Stars	31	7	.000	0	0	0	0	0	0	0	3	0	0	9	0
1995	Yokohama Bay Stars	47	8	.125	0	1	0	0	0	2	0	5	0	1	3	0
1996	Yokohama Bay Stars	39	4	.000	0	0	0	0	0	0	0	3	0	1	3	1
1997	Yokohama Bay Stars	49	5	.000	0	0	0	0	0	0	1	5	0	1	4	0
1998	Yokohama Bay Stars	51	9	.000	0	0	0	0	0	0	0	8	0	2	5	0
1999	Yokohama Bay Stars	23	2	.000	0	0	0	0	0	0	0	0	0	0	5	0
	TOTALS (10 YEARS)	415	95	.116	2	11	2	0	0	5	4	48	0	17	69	5

JAPAN SERIES

PITCHING

YEAR	TEAM	W	L	G	GS	CG	ShO	Sv	IP	H	R	ER	ERA	BB	SO
1998	Yokohama Bay Stars	0	0	3	0	0	0	1	3.1	1	1	1	2.70	2	1
TOTALS (1 YEAR)		0	0	3	0	0	0	1	3.1	1	1	1	2.70	2	1

BATTING

											FIELDING		
YEAR	TEAM	G	AB	R	H	2B	3B	HR	RBI	SO	BB	SB	
1998	Yokohama Bay Stars	3	0	.000	0	0	0	0	0	0	0	0	
TOTALS (1 YEAR)		3	0	.000	0	0	0	0	0	0	0	0	

PO	A	E
0	1	0
0	1	0

ALL-STAR GAMES

PITCHING

YEAR	TEAM	W	L	G	GS	CG	ShO	Sv	IP	H	R	ER	ERA	BB	SO
1992	Central League	0	0	2	0	0	0	1	3	1	1	1	3.00	1	3
1993	Central League	0	0	1	0	0	0	0	1.1	2	0	0	0.00	0	2
1995	Central League	0	0	1	1	0	0	0	2	3	1	1	4.50	0	4
1996	Central League	0	0	2	0	0	0	0	2	1	0	0	0.00	1	5
1997	Central League	0	0	1	0	0	0	1	1	0	0	0	0.00	0	1
1998	Central League	0	0	1	0	0	0	0	1	1	0	0	0.00	0	2
1999	Central League	0	0	1	0	0	0	0	1	3	1	1	9.00	0	1
TOTALS (7 YEARS)		0	0	9	1	0	0	2	11.1	11	3	3	2.38	2	18

YEAR	TEAM	BATTING												FIELDING		
		G	AB	Avg	R	H	2B	3B	HR	RBI	BB	SO	SB	PO	A	E
1992	Central League	2	0	.000	0	0	0	0	0	0	0	0	0	0	0	0
1993	Central League	1	0	.000	0	0	0	0	0	0	0	0	0	0	0	0
1995	Central League	1	0	.000	0	0	0	0	0	0	0	0	0	0	0	0
1996	Central League	2	0	.000	0	0	0	0	0	0	0	0	0	0	0	0
1997	Central League	1	0	.000	0	0	0	0	0	0	0	0	0	0	0	0
1998	Central League	1	0	.000	0	0	0	0	0	0	0	0	0	0	0	0
1999	Central League	1	0	.000	0	0	0	0	0	0	0	0	0	0	0	0
TOTALS (7 YEARS)		9	0	.000	0	0	0	0	0	0	0	0	0	0	0	0

Tsuyoshi Shinjo

HONORS
- Outfielder on C.L. All-Star team (1993, 2000)
- Won C.L. Gold Glove as outfielder (1993–1994, 1996–2000)

RECORDS
- Shares single-game record for most at-bats—6 (July 23, 2000)

REGULAR SEASON

YEAR	TEAM	BATTING												FIELDING		
		G	AB	Avg	R	H	2B	3B	HR	RBI	BB	SO	SB	PO	A	E
1991	Hanshin Tigers	13	17	.118	1	2	0	0	0	0	0	3	0	0	10	3
1992	Hanshin Tigers	95	353	.278	39	98	16	3	11	46	18	73	5	149	73	7
1993	Hanshin Tigers	102	408	.257	50	105	13	1	23	62	20	91	13	236	13	6
1994	Hanshin Tigers	122	466	.251	54	117	23	7	17	68	30	93	7	289	4	1
1995	Hanshin Tigers	87	311	.225	34	70	15	3	7	37	26	76	6	206	5	3
1996	Hanshin Tigers	113	408	.238	55	97	16	4	19	66	55	106	2	248	6	4
1997	Hanshin Tigers	136	482	.232	62	112	17	3	20	68	44	120	8	276	13	6
1998	Hanshin Tigers	132	414	.222	39	92	21	3	6	27	25	65	1	268	12	4
1999	Hanshin Tigers	123	471	.255	53	120	21	7	14	58	23	72	8	247	9	3
2000	Hanshin Tigers	131	511	.278	71	142	23	1	28	85	32	93	15	251	11	3
TOTALS (10 YEARS)		54	3841	.249	458	955	165	32	145	518	273	792	65	2176	156	40

ALL-STAR GAMES

RECORDS: Shares single-game record for most at-bats—6 (July 23, 2000).
NOTES: Named Most Valuable Player (July 27, 1999, Game 3).

YEAR	TEAM	BATTING												FIELDING		
		G	AB	Avg	R	H	2B	3B	HR	RBI	BB	SO	SB	PO	A	E
1994	Central League	2	2	.000	1	0	0	0	0	0	1	0	2	0	1	0
1997	Central League	2	2	.000	0	0	0	0	0	0	0	1	0	1	0	0
1999	Central League	3	9	.556	2	5	1	0	1	3	0	1	0	4	1	0
2000	Central League	3	13	.385	3	5	1	0	1	1	0	1	0	4	1	0
TOTALS (4 YEARS)		10	26	.385	6	10	2	0	2	4	1	3	2	9	3	0

Masato Yoshii

RECORDS
- Shares C.L. single-inning record for most bases on balls—5 (August 6, 1995, third inning)

TITLES
- Pacific League "Fireman of the Year" (1998)

REGULAR SEASON

PITCHING

YEAR	TEAM	W	L	G	GS	CG	ShO	Sv	IP	H	R	ER	ERA	BB	SO
1985	Kintetsu Buffaloes	0	1	2	1	0	0	0	3	6	9	7	21.00	3	1
1986	Kintetsu Buffaloes	0	0	2	0	0	0	0	2.1	10	7	6	23.14	2	2
1987	Kintetsu Buffaloes	2	1	13	2	1	0	0	36	45	21	19	4.75	12	23
1988	Kintetsu Buffaloes	10	2	50	0	0	0	24	80.1	76	27	24	2.69	27	44
1989	Kintetsu Buffaloes	5	5	47	0	0	0	20	84.1	77	28	28	2.99	37	44
1990	Kintetsu Buffaloes	8	9	45	2	0	0	15	74.1	80	29	28	3.39	30	55
1991	Kintetsu Buffaloes	2	1	21	0	0	0	2	26.1	30	11	10	3.42	6	13
1992	Kintetsu Buffaloes	1	0	9	0	0	0	0	11.2	10	3	3	2.31	2	4
1993	Kintetsu Buffaloes	5	5	22	13	2	1	0	104.2	100	38	31	2.67	25	66
1994	Kintetsu Buffaloes	7	7	21	19	2	0	0	97	118	69	59	5.47	37	42
1995	Yakult Swallows	10	7	25	22	7	2	0	147.1	127	53	51	3.12	39	91
1996	Yakult Swallows	10	7	25	24	9	1	0	180.1	177	69	65	3.24	47	146
1997	Yakult Swallows	13	6	28	26	6	2	0	174.1	149	61	58	2.99	48	104
	TOTALS (13 YEARS)	73	51	310	109	27	6	61	1022	1005	425	389	3.43	315	634

YEAR	TEAM	BATTING												FIELDING		
		G	AB	Avg	R	H	2B	3B	HR	RBI	BB	SO	SB	PO	A	E
1985	Kintetsu Buffaloes	2	0	.000	0	0	0	0	0	0	0	0	0	1	1	0
1986	Kintetsu Buffaloes	2	0	.000	0	0	0	0	0	0	0	0	0	0	1	0
1987	Kintetsu Buffaloes	15	0	.000	0	0	0	0	0	0	0	0	0	4	7	1
1988	Kintetsu Buffaloes	50	0	.000	0	0	0	0	0	0	0	0	0	4	23	0
1989	Kintetsu Buffaloes	47	0	.000	0	0	0	0	0	0	0	0	0	2	17	0
1990	Kintetsu Buffaloes	46	0	.000	0	0	0	0	0	0	0	0	0	3	15	0
1991	Kintetsu Buffaloes	21	0	.000	0	0	0	0	0	0	0	0	0	1	11	0
1992	Kintetsu Buffaloes	9	0	.000	0	0	0	0	0	0	0	0	0	1	4	0
1993	Kintetsu Buffaloes	36	0	.000	0	0	0	0	0	0	0	0	0	9	20	2
1994	Kintetsu Buffaloes	21	0	.000	0	0	0	0	0	0	0	0	0	6	21	0
1995	Yakult Swallows	34	48	.042	0	2	0	0	0	1	0	22	0	3	21	0
1996	Yakult Swallows	26	62	.097	3	6	0	0	0	2	1	31	0	10	27	0
1997	Yakult Swallows	35	56	.179	4	10	1	0	0	7	0	17	0	12	29	0
TOTALS (13 YEARS)		344	166	.108	7	18	1	0	0	10	1	70	0	56	197	3

JAPAN SERIES

PITCHING

YEAR	TEAM	W	L	G	GS	CG	ShO	Sv	IP	H	R	ER	ERA	BB	SO
1989	Kintetsu Buffaloes	0	0	5	0	0	0	1	8.2	5	6	6	6.23	4	6
1995	Yakult Swallows	0	0	1	1	0	0	0	5	3	1	1	1.80	4	3
1997	Yakult Swallows	0	0	1	1	0	0	0	4	7	3	3	6.75	2	3
TOTALS (3 YEARS)		0	0	7	2	0	0	1	17.2	15	10	10	5.09	10	12

BATTING

YEAR	TEAM	G	AB	Avg	R	H	2B	3B	HR	RBI	BB	SO	SB	PO	A	E
1989	Kintetsu Buffaloes	5	0	.000	0	0	0	0	0	0	0	0	0	0	3	0
1995	Yakult Swallows	1	1	1.000	0	1	1	0	0	0	0	0	0	0	0	0
1997	Yakult Swallows	1	1	.000	1	0	0	0	0	0	0	0	0	0	2	0
TOTALS (3 YEARS)		7	2	.500	1	1	1	0	0	0	0	0	0	0	5	0

(FIELDING: PO, A, E)

ALL-STAR GAMES

PITCHING

YEAR	TEAM	W	L	G	GS	CG	ShO	Sv	IP	H	R	ER	ERA	BB	SO
1988	Pacific League	0	0	1	0	0	0	0	1	1	1	1	9.00	1	1
1995	Central League	0	0	1	0	0	0	0	1	0	1	1	0.00	0	2
1996	Central League	0	0	1	0	0	0	0	2	2	0	0	0.00	1	0
1997	Central League	0	0	1	0	0	0	0	3	3	2	2	6.00	0	1
TOTALS (4 YEARS)		0	0	4	0	0	0	0	7	6	3	3	3.86	2	4

BATTING / FIELDING

YEAR	TEAM	G	AB	Avg	R	H	2B	3B	HR	RBI	BB	SO	SB	PO	A	E
1988	Pacific League	1	0	.000	0	0	0	0	0	0	0	0	0	0	0	0
1995	Central League	1	0	.000	0	0	0	0	0	0	0	0	0	0	0	0
1996	Central League	1	0	.000	0	0	0	0	0	0	0	0	0	0	0	0
1997	Central League	1	0	.000	0	0	0	0	0	0	0	0	0	0	1	0
TOTALS (4 YEARS)		4	0	.000	0	0	0	0	0	0	0	0	0	0	0	0

MORE WINNING SPORTS BOOKS
FROM ST. MARTIN'S PAPERBACKS

MARCUS:
The Autobiography of Marcus Allen,
with Carlton Stowers
From his triumphant rise to football stardom to his friendship with O.J. Simpson, get the real story—in his own words—on Heisman Trophy winner Marcus Allen.

HANG TIME:
Days and Dreams with Michael Jordan,
by Bob Greene
Journalist and bestselling author Bob Greene follows sports legend Michael Jordan for two seasons with the Chicago Bulls, and uncovers some amazing things about the athlete—and the man.

MICHAEL JORDAN, by Mitchell Krugel
A head-to-toe portrait of basketball's phenomenal Michael Jordan—on and off the court, in intimate detail.

THIS GAME'S THE BEST!
So Why Don't They Quit Screwing With It?
by George Karl with Don Yaeger
The fiery, funny, outspoken head coach of the Seattle Supersonics cuts loose on the sport of basketball and all its players.

AVAILABLE WHEREVER BOOKS ARE SOLD
FROM ST. MARTIN'S PAPERBACKS